V.J.W

THE LOST
NEW ENGLAND NINE

All the best!

Will Anderson

"Boston is the luckiest baseball spot on earth, for it has never lost a world's series."

The New York Times of September 12, 1918, reporting on the sixth and final game of the World Series of 1918

THE BEST OF NEW ENGLAND'S FORGOTTEN BALLPLAYERS

THE LOST NEW ENGLAND NINE

by WILL ANDERSON

ANDERSON & SONS' PUBLISHING CO.

34 PARK STREET

BATH, MAINE 04530

(207) 442-7459

www.andersonandsons.com

A MAINE-OWNED AND OPERATED COMPANY SINCE 1987

Other Books by Will Anderson

Beers, Breweries & Breweriana (1969)
The Beer Book (1973)
The Beer Poster Book (1977)
Beer, New England (1988)
New England Roadside Delights (1989)
Mid-Atlantic Roadside Delights (1991)
Was Baseball Really Invented in Maine? (1992)
Good Old Maine (1993)
More Good Old Maine (1995)
The Great State of Maine Beer Book (1996)
Where Have You Gone, Starlight Cafe? (1998)
You Auto See Maine (1999)
Lost Diners and Roadside Restaurants of New England and New York (2001)
Those Were the Days (2002)

Will Anderson 1940 –

1. Baseball   2. New England   3. History
ISBN 1-893804-03-8

Typesetting/Editorial Assistance by Brian Stanton, Bath, Maine
Printed by Spectrum Printing & Graphics, Auburn, Maine
Cover Lamination by New England Finishing, Holyoke, Massachusetts
Bound by Optimum Bindery Services of New England, Nashua, New Hampshire
Text Stock: 100 lb. Aero Gloss, Sappi North America, Westbrook, Maine
Cover Concept: Dick Hubsch, Carmel, New York
Cover Art: Olin Williams, Wells, Maine

Cover views, left to right: Bill Carrigan, Larry Gardner, Frank "Shanty" Hogan, Stuffy McInnis

TABLE OF CONTENTS

ACKNOWLEDGMENTS

In the researching and writing of THE LOST NEW ENGLAND NINE
I've had the assistance of many, many fine folks.
I'd like to especially thank:

George Altison, Boston Braves Historical Association, Marlborough, Mass. • Peter D. Bachelder, Ellsworth, Me. • Bob Brady, Boston Braves Historical Association, Braintree, Mass. • W.C. Burdick, National Baseball Hall of Fame, Cooperstown, N.Y. • Ray Collins, Jr., Middlebury, Vt. • Joe Connolly, Jr., Manville R.I. • Timothy Connor, Cambridge Public Library, Cambridge, Mass. • Dean Corner, Patten Free Library, Bath, Me. • Rae B. Cousins, Cranston Public Library, Cranston, R.I. • Jason Fenimore, Goodall Library, Sanford, Me. • Bill Francis, National Baseball Hall of Fame, Cooperstown, N.Y. • Pat Garrity, Somerville High School, Somerville, Mass. • Augie Helms, Garwood, N.J. • Midge Landry, Lowell, Mass. • Bernie Littlefield, Danvers, Mass. • Michael Lord, Androscoggin Historical Society, Auburn, Me. • Debbie Matson, Boston Red Sox, Boston, Mass. • Judith E. Mayer, National Baseball Hall of Fame, Cooperstown, N.Y. • Bob Pacios, Auburn-Lewiston Sports Hall of Fame, Lewiston, Me. • Marlene Parent, Springvale Public Library, Springvale, Me. • Randy Roberts, Warren, Me. • Gabriel Schechter, National Baseball Hall of Fame, Cooperstown, N.Y. • Aaron Schmidt, Boston Public Library, Boston, Mass. • Dick Shaw, Bangor, Me. • Thomas F. Shehan, Sr., Scarborough, Me. • Jim Starkman, Pittsford, N.Y. • Bryan Strniste, Woonsocket Harris Public Library, Woonsocket, R.I. • Bob Weaver, Westport, Me. • Tim Wiles, National Baseball Hall of Fame, Cooperstown, N.Y.

And a VERY SPECIAL THANKS to my wife Catherine, for being my wife Catherine, and to Norm "The Archives" Furrow of Bath, Maine for allowing me the full usage of his marvelous collection of Maine and New England baseball memorabilia. When I needed help, Norm – and his faithful pooch, Homer – just about always came through like a Walter Johnson fastball.

DEDICATION

To my sons, Carl and Curt,

From Pittsfield, Pawtucket and New Britain, to OOB,
Waterbury, Bristol, Norwich, Portland, Lowell, and,
of course, Fenway, too...thanks for all the wondrous
times that I've shared with you.

The Ultimate Dream

To make the bigs. That was and is the dream. To make the bigs with your "hometown" team. That's *the* Ultimate Dream. For most of these six states we call New England that hometown team was and is Boston. The Hub. The Athens of America. And the home of the Boston Red Stockings/Beaneaters/Doves/Rustlers/Bees/Braves from 1876 to 1952, and the Boston Somersets/Pilgrims/Puritans/Red Sox from 1901 until, hopefully, forever.

Those who achieved this Ultimate Dream – to be from New England and to have played for New England – include such greats as Carlton Fisk (Red Sox), Rabbit Maranville (Braves), Jimmy Piersall (Red Sox), Billy Monbouquette (Red Sox), Tony Conigliaro (Red Sox), and Walt "The Moosup Moose" Dropo (Red Sox). Some are enshrined in Cooperstown. Some are not. All are remembered.

There is another tier of ballplayers, however, who achieved – and did well at – that Ultimate Dream, too. But who are now largely forgotten. This book is about them.

Looking Back

I grew up, I must admit, in Yonkers, New York. Yonkers is not New England. But it is east of the Hudson. More important, it was a baseball town. As a kid, in the years around 1950, we would play about two weeks of football in the fall.

No basketball. And certainly no hockey. Hockey was something they played in foreign countries. Or maybe upstate. But never in Yonkers.

We'd play baseball. Actually, mostly stickball. Our home field was an old abandoned tennis court with a high wire-mesh fence surrounding it. It was sort of like The Green Monster, except you could see through it. Looking at tennis courts now, I realize our field wasn't very big. But when we were ten or so it might as well have been Braves Field or the Polo Grounds or Fenway Park.

Our bat was a sawed-off broom or shovel handle, or a clothes rod we'd "borrowed" from a construction job in the vicinity. We'd use an old tennis ball – not too terribly difficult to find around an old tennis court – or, occasionally, a shiny new Spaldeen.

Our most important piece of "equipment," however, was probably desire. There was no Little League. We played because we *wanted* to; not because it was Tuesday or Thursday and we were *supposed* to. And when we weren't playing we were busy collecting baseball cards. We started with the little Bowman black and whites and then moved on to the more exotic Topps' models. We, of course, each had our favorite team(s) and our favorite player(s). Most of my friends were Yankee fans. They liked Joe D. or Gene Woodling or "The Chief," Allie Reynolds, or, of course, the Mick.

INTRODUCTION

There were a few Dodger fans. Their favorites were Duke Snider or Gil Hodges or Pee Wee Reese, or the "Oisk," Carl Erskine. Then there was my pal, Joe Alutto. Joe and his family had moved up from the City. Joe was the only Giant fan I knew. His favorite – no surprise here – was Willie Mays. Plus Joe liked Bobby Thomson. After 1951 what Giant fan didn't?

I began life, I am ashamed to say, as a Yankee fan. I especially liked Eddie Lopat. He had a fast ball that, as the saying goes, wouldn't break a pane of glass. But he could and would outsmart you with his "stuff." And he'd win his 17 or 18 or 21 games a year. "Steady Eddie." I soon realized, however, that the Yankees didn't need my support. They always won. And if they didn't, they'd go out and buy or trade for the likes of a Johnny Mize or a Johnny Hopp or a Johnny Sain. That bothered me. It was like they were greedy.

In the summer of 1953, when I was going on 13, I made a momentous decision. I became a Pittsburgh Pirate fan. The first on the block. I chose the Pirates because they were terrible. (They were 42-112 in 1952; 50-104 in 1953.). They "needed" me. I also chose them because my cousin, Eddie McCarrick – *my first cousin*, Eddie McCarrick, I was always proud to point out – was a Pirate scout. He'd signed the O'Brien twins, Eddie and Johnny. (He also signed Mario Cuomo, who played a season in the Pirate farm system before giving up baseball in favor of politics.). Most of all, the Pirates had a young leftfielder – who would later play third and first, too – named Frank Thomas. In his first full season with the Bucs, 1953, Frank would end up slamming 30 homers and driving in 102 runs for a team that had precious few runners on base to drive in. Frank Thomas – not, of course, today's Frank Thomas of the White Sox – became my idol. I would read the Pirates' box score religiously every day. How many hits did Frank get? How many RBIs? If he got a hit it was as if I'd gotten a hit. If he hit a home run it was as if I'd pulled a shot down the leftfield line myself.

I stuck with the Pirates and Frank Thomas until 1959, when my idol was traded to the Reds. Then I wandered. I rooted for no team. As long as the Yankees weren't winning, I was content. I also had no really favorite player. I liked Minnie Minoso for a while. I thought he had a "cool" name. I liked Gene Freese. I liked the way he'd knock down ground balls with his chest at third and then throw the runner out. He was a gritty guy. I hooked up with Frank Thomas again in 1962 when he was a member of the hapless original Mets. Only Frank wasn't hapless. In the Mets' inaugural year the veteran hit 34 homers and knocked in 94 runs. I was there, as well, rooting for Frank in 1964 when I lived briefly in Philadelphia and Frank found himself playing first for the Phillies. (He almost led them to their first pennant in 49 years, too). And when my first son was born in March of 1965 he was named Carl Thomas Anderson. There was never any doubt as to where the "Thomas" came from.

In 1970 I moved from New York to New England. To Newtown, Connecticut. It wasn't exactly Lowell or Worcester or Providence. It was, in fact, scarcely 15 miles over the New York/Connecticut state line. But it was New England. After drifting through the late sixties I became absorbed in baseball once again. I became a Red Sox fan. I can recall trying to convince the sportswriters at the nearby *Danbury News-Times* that they should write more on the Sox. They'd just laugh and say that western Connecticut was Yankees'/Mets' country.

I began to follow certain players again. I liked Rico Petrocelli. I rooted for Joe Lahoud (who was, after all, from Danbury) during his stay in a Boston uniform. I loved to watch Luis Tiant on the mound. He was such fun, what with all his twisting, turning, and gyrating. But it wasn't until Butch Hobson came on the Boston scene in 1976 that I found myself with a real favorite once more. Butch was my kind of guy. He certainly wasn't great (as Carl, who revered Carlton Fisk, was wont to point out). Not like Fisk. Or Yaz. Or Jim Rice. Or Fred Lynn. But he

was good. A steady RBI guy with a fair amount of home-run pop in his bat.

The Second String

This gets us back to the beginning. That this is a book that pays tribute to the good and the very good, rather than the great. To the "Second String" or "Junior Hall of Fame" players of the game, as Birdie Tebbetts (see page 127) once put it so well. Guys who, to partake of Cooperstown, drive there with their family, check into a motel, and buy a ticket.

Just like the rest of us.

This book is also dedicated to New England-born ballplayers. Guys from Yonkers need not apply. And, as it worked out, all six New England states are well represented within the book's pages. Each state, in fact, has at least one player on the starting team. I was glad of that.

To be included in the book, a player must have spent all or most of all his career in the twentieth century. Nineteenth-century rules were often just too inconsistent when compared to the rules of today.

And, to reiterate, a player must have spent all or a substantial portion of his seasons in the sun in either a Red Sox or a (Boston) Braves' uniform: to have been a part of that Ultimate Dream of being from New England/playing for New England. THE LOST NEW ENGLAND NINE, then, does not pay homage to those

INTRODUCTION

Johnny Moore, 1935

Vic Raschi, 1952

Whitey Witt, 1920

NEVER TO HAVE PLAYED FOR THE HOME TEAM

The three players pictured here – Johnny Moore, Vic Raschi, and Whitey Witt (real name: Ladislaw Waldermar Wittkowski) – were all fine ballplayers who were from New England but who, alas, never wore a Boston uniform. Moore (born in Waterbury, Connecticut on March 23, 1902/died in Bradenton, Florida on April 4, 1991) put in ten satisfying seasons with the Cubs, Reds, and Phillies, 1928-1937 and 1945, batting over .300 five times and finishing at .307 lifetime. Raschi (born in West Springfield, Massachusetts on March 28, 1919/died in Groveland, New York on October 14, 1988) was a top-notch moundsman for the Yankees, Cards, and Kansas City, 1946-1955. Nicknamed "The Springfield Rifle," he was 132-66 lifetime, for a remarkable .667 won-lost percentage. Witt (born in Orange, Massachusetts on September 28, 1895/died in Salem, New Jersey on July 14, 1988) patrolled the outfield for the Athletics, Yankees, and Dodgers, 1916-1926, hitting over .300 three times and finishing with a .287 lifetime mark.

Did each regret not having played for a team that called Boston home? You can almost be certain of it.

INTRODUCTION

many fine New England-born yesteryear ballplayers (defined here as having played some or all of their career prior to 1965) who had the misfortune to have never played for – or scarcely played for – the "home team." Red Rolfe, Whitey Witt, Bump Hadley, Vic Raschi, Tommy Corcoran, Wild Bill Donovan, Johnny Moore, Jack Burns, Bill Hunnefield, Matty McIntyre, Ray Fisher, Cy Perkins, Dick "Turk" Farrell, Jean Dubuc, Red Donahue, Danny Hoffman, Clyde "Sukey" Sukeforth, Jim Hegan, Ernie Johnson, Dick Donovan, Dickie McAuliffe, Tom Padden, Pete Castiglione, Spec "The Naugatuck Nugget" Shea, Eddie Waitkus (the inspiration for THE NATURAL), Dick Siebert, Kiddo Davis, Jack Sanford, Art Ditmar, Kitty Bransfield, Chuck Essegian, Bob Ganley, Eddie Mayo, Gene Hermanski, Joe Coleman (both father and son), Clem Labine, Blondy Ryan, Mike Lynch, Hugh "Losing Pitcher" Mulcahy, Rosy Ryan, Eddie Ainsmith, "Harvard Eddie" Grant, Billy Maloney, Wilbur Wood, Stu Miller, Rollie Sheldon, Stan Williams, Billy Gardner, Carlton Willey, Steve Blass, Lennie Merullo, and Joey Jay are all players who fall into this category.

And, once more, THE LOST NEW ENGLAND NINE is not an All-Time/All-Star New England Nine. It is not about Carlton Fisk, Pie Traynor, Gabby Hartnett, Nappy "The Woonsocket Wonder" Lajoie, Rabbit Maranville, Mickey Cochrane, Hugh Duffy, Tony C., Jack Chesbro, Leo Durocher, Connie Mack, Jimmy Piersall, Walt Dropo, or Wilbert "Uncle Robbie" Robinson.

Lastly, to be included within these pages a player must be largely unsung. Forgotten. Lost. If a past player can show up at a baseball card show, he is not lost. There are numerous New England-born former ballplayers who are knocked out of the book's batter's box because they played in a Boston uniform too recently to be categorized as forgotten. Included in this group are Phil Plantier, Billy Conigliaro, John Curtis, Rich Gale, Russ Gibson, Jeff "The Terminator" Reardon, Allen Ripley, Jerry Remy, Rich Gedman, Mike Ryan, and, of course, present-day Mo Vaughn, catching hopeful Steve Lomasney, and Framingham's Lou Merloni.

Enjoy THE LOST NEW ENGLAND NINE. I hope you agree that it applauds some players who should be applauded.

Postscript: THE LOST NEW ENGLAND NINE is really the The Lost New England Eleven. That's because there are two pitchers on the starting team. One righty. One lefty. Plus there's a manager. The baseball life story of each selectee is given, position by position, followed by a shorter tribute to a number of other worthy candidates at each position. They all have a meaningful share in New England baseball history.

FIRST BASE

John Phalen "Stuffy" McGinnis

If there's a ballplayer who should not be in this book, it's John Phalen "Stuffy" McGinnis. Stuffy hit a rock-solid .308 over 19 seasons in the bigs, was the anchor on Connie Mack's fabled $100,000 infield (so-called because Mr. Mack reputedly proclaimed he would not take $100,000 for it), held down first for the Red Sox the last time they won a World Series, and, using the small, almost-homemade gloves of yesteryear, set a bevy of fielding records, some of which still stand. Stuffy McGinnis should not be in this book simply because Stuffy McInnis should be in the Hall of Fame.

Born in Gloucester, Massachusetts on September 19, 1890, Stuffy McGinnis was a standout ballplayer in both grammar and high school. He was so good, in fact, that while still attending Gloucester High – where he earned recognition as probably the finest schoolboy shortstop in all of New England – Stuffy also suited up for strong semi-pro teams in Rockport and Beverly (Massachusetts). That was in 1906-1907. He then, in 1908, moved on to Haverhill in the New England League where he played, in the words of one local sportswriter, like a "bearcat." Another scribe, in the hyperbole of the day, wrote that the teenager, en route to a .301 average, "walloped the

sphere till it shrieked for mercy." Connie Mack, himself a native of the Bay State, learned of Stuffy in mid-1908 and wasted no time in signing the shortstop phenom to a Philadelphia contract. Mack, in fact, is said to have stated "There's a youngster that is bound to make good." The problem was that it was hard to make good with the Athletics because *they* were so good. The result: Stuffy spent the season of 1909 riding the Athletics' bench, getting into but 19 games. One of those 19, though, is well worthy of note. On April 12 of that long-ago season, the Athletics opened the world's first all concrete and steel stadium, Shibe Park. And playing shortstop for Connie Mack's charges that celebratory afternoon was Stuffy McInnis. The lad – he was not yet 19 – went one for four at bat and was errorless in the field as the Athletics humbled the Red Sox, 8-1, before 30,162 delighted home town fans.

Although he played well when called upon, 1910 was pretty much a repeat of 1909 for most of Stuffy's season. There was simply no way for the youngster to dislodge the veteran Jack Barry (see page 46) at short. Stuffy's break would come, though, in the form of a vicious spiking of Barry by Ty Cobb in a pennant-race encounter between the Athletics and the Tigers on September 21. Barry ended up on crutches and Stuffy found himself at shortstop. There he more than held his own, fielding well and finishing the season with a most impressive batting average of .301 in 38 games for the second-place A's.

Come 1911, though, and Stuffy was back on the bench. Then, on April 22, Jack Barry was injured once more. In stepped Stuffy, and with a vengeance. He hit safely in his first five games as a starter and just kept rolling from there. Against the Yankees on April 29 he went five for five, including a triple. Wrote *The New York Times* in reflecting upon the game's 10-6 run barrage: "The lion of the day's clouting was Jack McInnis, from Gloucester, Mass., and he's a whaler. Five hits out of five times up, and fielding the shortstopper's province with a fine tooth comb, it was a noble day's work for the Gloucester lad." In a contest versus the very same Yankees the next week, on May 4, the "Gloucester lad" did it again; this time going three for five with a home run as the Athletics trounced the Yanks, 13-4. There followed a three-game set against the Browns in which Stuffy – also called "the Gloucester whaler" by the press – went a rousing nine for 13. Through May 15 the "whaler" was knocking out the ball at a .455 clip, tops among all players in either league. A week later, through May 20, he'd upped that mark to .481, well atop all batters – and we *are* talking Cobb, Lajoie, Joe Jackson, Honus Wagner and Tris Speaker here – in both circuits. Jack Barry, meanwhile, was back on the mend and ready to go, leaving manager Mack with a problem: what to do with a player who's batting .481. His answer was to bench the aging – and slipping – Harry Davis at first.

So Stuffy became a firstbaseman. He would go on to hold down the initial sack in 1,995 big league games. And to become one of the greats at that position.

As for the Athletics, after a sluggish start the World Champs (they'd defeated the Cubs in the 1910 Series) settled into another pennant duel with Ty Cobb, Sam Crawford, Jim Delahanty and the rest of Detroit's best. Stuffy usually found himself in the number five slot in the Athletics' attack. That's because, although smallish at 5' 9" and 162 pounds, the Gloucesterman could wallop the ball. He was two for four with a double and a triple against St. Louis on June 13 and banged out homers against the Red Sox on both June 24 and June 27. His "shot" on the 27th, however, was more cleverness than clout. First up in the eighth inning in a game against the Red Sox, Stuffy took his stance in the batter's box and then proceeded to poke a warm-up toss from Sox hurler Ed Karger into the outfield while the Bosox flyhawks were still wending their way to their respective positions. Then Stuffy proceeded to trot around the bases for an inside-the-park roundtripper. In spite of some serious protesting by Sox manager Patsy Donovan, home plate ump Ben Egan allowed the "home run" to stand. That's because, in an attempt to speed up baseball, the American League powers-that-were had banned warm-up tosses. Therefore, reasoned Egan, Karger's toss was a real pitch and Stuffy's poke a real home run. The no warm-up rule was eventually abolished. But it stood on June 27, 1911…and you can bet

FIRST BASE

"Stuffy" came by his distinctive nickname when, as a youth, teammates and fans would shout "That's the stuff" when he would make one of his sparkling fielding plays or get a timely hit.

Stuffy chortled all the way around the bases and for years thereafter, too.

On July 3 and July 4 the Athletics and the Yankees played back-to-back doubleheaders. The A's took all four games…and moved into first as the Tigers split with Chicago (and Ty Cobb's longest-ever hitting streak, 41 games, came to its end). The last game of the two-day marathon was especially rewarding for the Mackmen: down 7-0 after the first inning, they clawed back to win, 11-9, in eleven innings. Stuffy contributed two singles, two walks, and a sacrifice fly to the cause. After the twinbill A's sweep, one New York sportswriter, at least, became a believer. Wrote he: "After seeing the Athletics in action here last week New York fans are thoroughly convinced that the National League pennant winner will have to spend a few days in Philadelphia next October…The Tigers are expected to keep in the race perhaps to the finish, but the most rabid follower of the Jennings clan (Ed. note: Hughie Jennings was Detroit's manager) would hardly put up any of the family furniture that the Tigers will nose out Mack's speedy aggregation."

Strong rest-of-July performances by Stuffy included a two-for-five (with a triple) outing in a 7-1 win over Cleveland on the seventh; a two-for-four (with a double) game over the Indians again, July 8; another two-for-four (with a double) game over the Tigers on July 28; and a two-for-three outing in an 11-8 win over the Bengals the next day, July 29. As August dawned the Tigers were back in first. The Athletics were in second. Such was not to remain the case. The beginning of the Tigers' downfall came in a doubleheader against the Red Sox on August 2. The Tigers dropped both games, while the Athletics were topping St. Louis, 3-0, with Stuffy contributing a double and a run scored. Two days later the Red Sox defeated the Tigers again, while the Athletics were taking a doubleheader from the reliably-hapless Browns. The two A's wins coupled with the Tigers' loss propelled Connie Mack and company into the AL top spot…where they would remain the rest of the season. The Tigers were good. The Athletics were better. It's difficult, after all, to topple a team that would end up with five .300-plus players in the starting line-up: Eddie Collins (.365); Frank "Home Run" Baker (.334); Danny Murphy (.329); Stuffy (.321); and Bris Lord (.310). The A's had pitching, too. "Colby Jack" Coombs won 28; Eddie Plank won 23; Charles "Chief" Bender took 17; while Cy Morgan kicked in with 15.

The Athletics' marvelous year – they would win 101 games against but 50 losses – was most definitely a team effort. Yet, perhaps because of his youth, Stuffy seemed to be singled out for more than a fair share of praise. A splendid example was *The New York Times* of September 12 after an A's 12-2 shellacking of the Yankees the day before: "Connie Mack's World Champions continued on their triumphant jaunt to Pennantville…The prospective champions of 1911 did nothing but hit. Every man on the team succeeded in getting at least one safe clout, and little McInnis, who gathered five (hits) in a row in one of the previous games between the same teams at the Hilltop this year, made a bold effort to repeat. On each of his first four trips to the plate he connected safely, and his fifth chance was productive of a slam to left field which would have been good for two bases but for a great running catch by (Guy) Zinn," the Yankee leftfielder. The praise

hit on his right wrist by a fast ball from the Tigers' George Mullin. At first thought to be of little consequence, the wounded wrist did not heal well. The result was that Stuffy played the bench for the remainder of the season and for the World Series as well. Stuff was replaced in the Athletics' line-up by his predecessor, Harry Davis, and watched from the dugout as his teammates, in the Series, handily defeated

"DO YOU BELONG TO THE CLUB?"

Sometimes Connie Mack liked to wander about before a game. He did some of that up until just before game time for contest number three of the 1913 World Series at the Polo Grounds. Then, coming onto the field from the team clubhouse, he was stopped by a park security guard. "I want to go to the visitors' bench," explained Connie. "Do you belong to the club?" asked the guard. "No," replied Connie, "the club belongs to me."

continued the next day, as the Athletics posted another win, 10-1, over the New Yorkers: "The Athletics put up a brilliant fielding game. McGinnis, at first, led in the dazzling plays with a spectacular stop of a sizzling grounder, a one-handed catch of a lofty toss by Barry, and the capture of a difficult foul fly."

Stuffy's splendid play, unfortunately, ended for the season on September 25 when he was

John McGraw and the mighty New York Giants four games to two. The somewhat sentimental Connie Mack did, though, send his rookie star into the Series in the very last inning of game six. With two away Stuffy took over at first from Davis, and he had the distinction of recording the game's last out when Giant catcher Art Wilson hit a grounder to A's thirdbaseman Home Run Baker, who fired the ball across the diamond to the young man from Gloucester. It was a nice touch.

By the spring of 1912 Stuffy and his wrist were both raring to go. Commented one writer, tongue in cheek, after seeing the Athletics' firstbaseman in action against the Yankees in late April: "Stuffy McInnis has made six hits in two games, two of them triples. His sore wrist is almost better." And one of the triples, it might be added, was described as having been hit so hard "that it looked as if it was going to tear the pickets off the fence."

A highlight – of sorts – in Stuffy's career was undoubtedly a game played in Philadelphia on May 18. It seems that, three days previous, Ty Cobb had gone into the stands in New York to "talk things over" with a fan who'd been heckling him. (Ed. note: Cobb, never known for a sunny disposition, had actually beaten the fan up). American League president Ban Johnson, deeming such action entirely inappropriate, suspended Cobb indefinitely. Cobb's teammates – though the Georgia Peach was hardly a favorite among his fellow Tigers – responded by vowing to go on strike on May 18 if Cobb's suspension wasn't lifted. Not wishing to pay the $5,000.00 fine levied for a no-show game, Detroit owner Frank Navin ordered Tiger manager Hughie Jennings to round up a substitute team. The result, with candidates plucked right out of the Shibe Park grandstand, was a disaster. A college hurler by the name of Aloysius Travers went the route for the "new Tigers," losing by a 24-2 margin. Eddie Collins got five hits. A's centerfielder

Amos Strunk got four. Stuffy got three. It was a game that, it is safe to say, was truly unique: like batting practice…but for real.

The Athletics, in 1912, could have used a few more games à la May 18. The defending World Champs played well, but both they and the Tigers slipped from 1911. There were even rumors that the Detroit team might be moved to Baltimore. The teams to beat in 1912 were not the A's or the Tigers. The teams to beat were the red-hot Red Sox and, surprise, the Senators. The best Connie's crew could do was battle it out with Clark Griffith's Washington club for the number two spot in the standings.

Stuffy, though, enjoyed what would be the best offensive season of his long career. He upped his average to .327, banged out a career-high 13 triples, and knocked in over 100 runs – 101, to be exact – for the only time in his 19 seasons of play. He stole 27 bases and scored 83 runs, both high-water marks as well. Standout games included a three-for-four performance in an 8-6 victory over the White Sox on May 15; a two-for-four-with-a-double afternoon vs. Detroit on July 19; and a three-for-four outing, again with a double and again against Detroit, on July 20. Then there was August 14. Talk about an afternoon not easily forgotten. All Stuffy did, in a doubleheader win over the Indians, 8-3 and 2-0, was clout two home runs, drive in three tallies and score twice in the first game, and then go three for four with a double and a run scored in the nightcap. And, as if frosting on the cake, the twin win, coupled with a Washington loss, sent the Athletics back

FIRST BASE

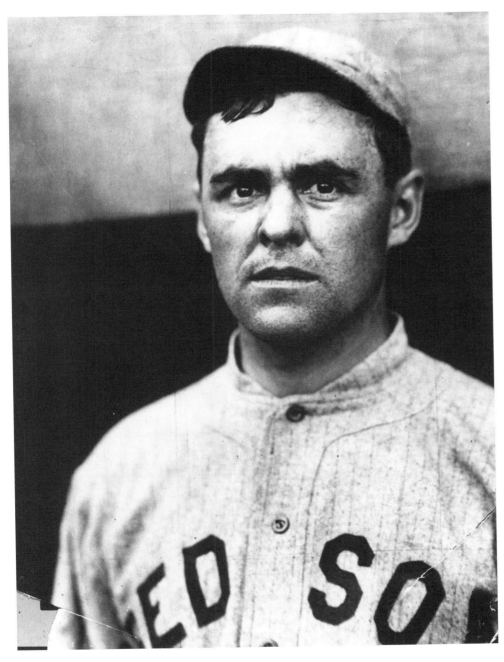

After nine seasons with Connie Mack's Philadelphia Athletics, Stuffy was traded to the Red Sox in January of 1918. He would go on to enjoy four very satisfying seasons with the boys of Fenway; was a key ingredient in the Sox success in the 1918 World Series.

Circa 1918 photo

into second place. As it all turned out, however, the Senators would reclaim second and hold it through season's end. The Athletics, World Champions in 1911, finished a disappointing third in 1912.

In terms of personal statistics Stuffy's 1913 was not very different than his 1912. He batted exactly one point lower – .326 instead of .327 – while dipping to 90 RBIs and 79 runs scored, both still highly respectable. And his stolen base count fell from 27 to 16. It was in terms of team success that 1913 differed greatly. The Red Sox fell to fourth. Cleveland moved from fifth to third. The Senators held fast in second. And the A's leapfrogged to the top. It was a convincing leap: there was little drama in the way of a pennant race. By August 1, the Athletics had things pretty much nailed down. By September 1, there was no doubt about it. It could almost be said, in fact, that the most noteworthy happening for the Mackmen in September came on the fourth. The Red Sox arrived in Philadelphia for a doubleheader. But their uniforms did not. What to do? The answer: the Bosox suited up in the A's away uniforms. It must have seemed an odd spectacle: the Athletics against the Athletics.

The World Series, as it had in 1905 and 1911, pitted the Athletics against the New York Giants. Noted - and often controversial (see page 53) – sportswriter and baseball analyst Hugh Fullerton predicted that there was a "Promise of (the) Fiercest and Most Exciting Championship Struggle Ever Seen." Mr. Fullerton was misinformed. The Athletics took a quick four out of five. The Giants' sole win came in the second game when their ace, Christy Mathewson, held the A's to eight hits in a 3-0 ten-inning shutout. Apart from Matty's performance the Mackmen had it all over the McGrawmen. Frank "Home Run" Baker and Eddie Collins both hit over .400 for Philadelphia while catcher Wally Schang pitched in with a .357 mark and Jack Barry saw an even .300. Stuffy was a disappointing two for 17 (which works out to .118). But his defensive skills were as pronounced as ever and, even with just two safeties, he managed to score two runs and knock in two. The Athletics were World Champs. And so was Stuffy.

Nineteen-fourteen was a year of dissension in the grand old game. A third major league, the Federal League, had been formed and its agents were out to requisition as many American and National League players as possible. Big money was offered. And a number of the A's let it be known that they were interested. Connie Mack was prone to say on more than one occasion that 1914 was the baseball year he liked the least.

In spite of all the uncertainties, though, the Athletics enjoyed a whale of a season. They wrestled first from the Tigers in late May, fought off a Red Sox comeback in September, and went on to take top billing quite handily. The team's key ingredients remained unchanged: the "$100,000 infield" of Baker, Barry, Collins, and Stuffy; Wally Schang behind the plate; and Eddie Plank and Chief Bender (aided by Bullet Joe Bush, Herb Pennock, and

FIRST BASE

Rube Bressler) on the mound. Stuffy's .314 was bettered on the team only by Eddie Collins' .344 and Frank Baker's .319. His 95 RBIs were bettered only by Baker's 97.

Then, though, came the World Series. From the Athletics' point of view, the less said about the Series of 1914 the better. (Ed. note: for the take on the A's worthy opponents, the "Miracle Braves," see pages 100-103). Heavily favored to repeat as World Champions, the Athletics sputtered and fell in four straight games. Eddie Collins hit .214. Frank "Home Run" Baker hit .250 (with no home runs). Jack Barry hit .071. Stuffy hit .143. His highlight probably arrived in game one when he drew a walk and then came around to score on a shot to right by Amos Strunk. The Athletics would score no more runs that game and only five more times in the remaining three games.

As disappointing as the sweep was for Philadelphia fans, it was far preferable to what they would witness over the next dozen seasons. Connie Mack was disgusted. With the raids from the Federal League. With his team's dreadful performance against the Braves. Rumors he was going to break up the team began to circulate almost as soon as the last Series' pitch had crossed the plate. Then rumors became facts. The first player to go was star secondbaseman Eddie Collins, sold to the White Sox for $50,000 on December 8. Future Hall-of-Fame moundsmen Eddie Plank and Chief Bender were released. Eventually the entire starting team would be sold or traded away. And the Athletics would descend into the lower levels of the American League for over a decade.

It may have been because he was a fellow New Englander. It may have been because he yet had a plentitude of playing time on his side. For whatever reason, Connie Mack kept Stuffy on the Athletics through 1917. The press called him "The Last of the Mohicans," because he was the last of the 1914 team to go elsewhere. Elsewhere, though, would almost certainly have been far more satisfying than the riches-to-rags scenario Stuff witnessed after the 1914 season. While his batting average certainly remained healthy – he repeated with .314 in 1915, fell to .295 in 1916, bounced back to .303 in 1917 – the team did not. The team plummeted. From first, with a 99-53 record in 1914, the Athletics plunged to 43-109 and dead last in 1915. Nineteen-sixteen just got worse. The team won but 36 games. The entire season. In 1917 they "jumped" to 55-98, still good enough for only last place.

In January of 1918 the inevitable happened: the last of the great Athletics' 1910-1914 dynasty ceased to be an Athletic. Stuffy was traded to the Red Sox. But not for money: for fellow players, and some good ones at that. To get Stuffy the Sox gave up thirdbaseman Larry Gardner (an all-time Bosox great: see pages 48-59), veteran outfielder Clarence "Tilly" Walker, and second-string catcher Forrest "Hick" Cady.

As events would have it, the Red Sox' first opponents for the season of 1918 were Stuffy's former team, the Athletics. Stuffy welcomed them to Fenway by going two for four in both of the first games of the series, April 16 and April 17. In the first encounter he also scored the game's only run as Sox submariner Carl Mays shut out the A's, 1-0. He then scored two times in game number two as the Sox again took the Athletics, this time 5-4. It was good to be back on a winning ball club.

At the outset of the 1918 campaign, however, the league's best firstbaseman found himself playing third. With Larry Gardner gone, the Sox' new manager, Ed Barrow, decided an experiment was in order. He positioned Stuff at the hot corner and veteran Dick Hoblitzell at first. It worked fine with respect to Stuffy. As *The New York Times* wrote of the experiment: "Stuffy seems to be one of those players who can play anywhere with grace and ease." With Hoblitzell, though, it was a different story. The ten-year veteran was struggling below .200 when manager Barrow moved Stuffy back to first on May 11.

Dates of note in that long-ago Championship season would include May 18. It was not until that day that the Red Sox, playing against the Tigers, hit their first home run of the summer. And it wasn't hit by the Babe, either. It was hit by centerfield star Harry Hooper. The team would go on to hit a grand total of 14 for the season, with the Bambino clouting a league-leading eleven of them.

In late June, after cruising along in the AL top spot since opening day, the Red Sox suddenly found themselves challenged by both the Yankees and the Indians. First to arrive were the Yankees. By taking three out of four from the Sox, June 24 - June 27, the New Yorkers were suddenly perched in first. But not for long. By June 30 they were back in second as George Herman hit a towering two-run shot against the Senators and the Sox won, 5-1. Stuffy kicked in with two hits in five trips to the plate. The Yanks, however, bounced right back and, amid rumors that the Babe was going to jump the Red Sox to work in a wartime ship-building plant, held it until early July. Next in line came Tris Speaker, Stanley Coveleski, and the rest of the Indians. By sweeping both ends of a July 4 doubleheader from the Browns, *they* moved into first.

On July 6, though, the Sox defeated the Tribe, 5-4, and moved on top once more. Ruth, playing every day in addition to taking his customary turn on the mound, was once more the deciding factor. He blasted a two-run triple in the sixth to put Boston ahead.

After their topsy-turvy late June/early July, the Red Sox settled in first to stay. With the Bambino getting extra-base hits as if he owned the league's pitchers, it was not terribly difficult for the Hub Hose to pile up victory after victory. Other players, of course, contributed to the team's success as well. A pair of wins in which Stuffy was instrumental came against Detroit on July 19 and July 20. Stuffy went four for four with 21 putouts in a 5-1 Boston victory ("McGinnis's hitting and fielding were remarkable," wrote *The New York Times*) in game one, and then chimed in with a double and single in four at-bats in game two. Wrote *The Times* of that game: "The batting and fielding of (Tiger shortstop Donnie) Bush and McGinnis were features." Another strong game for our favorite firstsacker came against the Brownies in St. Louis on July 31. Stuffy was two for four with a triple, sacrifice fly, and two runs scored in an 8-4 Red Sox win.

By early August it was obvious that the 1918 season was going to be shortened because of the war. August, from a pennant race point of view, became September. With time running out, the Indians, in second place most of the summer, knew they had to make their move. Their chance came on August 17-20 when they squared off in a three-game series in Boston. The Tribe, however, just didn't have it. The Sox took the first two, 4-2 and 4-0. Bosox ace Sad Sam Jones held Cleveland to a pair of singles in game two while the Babe did the honors with a five-hitter in the opener. Stuffy, who'd been mired in a slump and who would end the season with a disappointing .272 mark, nevertheless contributed six hits in ten at-bats in the Cleveland downfall. The Indians did take number three, 8-1, but it was too late. They were out of it.

So it was on to yet another World's Championship Series for the Red Sox. Their fourth in seven years. It was yet to be boring…but it sure was becoming routine. Their worthy opponents: the sizzling Chicago Cubs. The Cubbies, managed by Cambridge-native Fred Mitchell (See page 134), had run away with the National League pennant, and, with a pitching staff that radiated around Jim "Hippo" Vaughn (22-10; the league's only 20-game winner in the war-shortened season), George "Lefty" Tyler (19-9; the Pride of Derry, New Hampshire), and Claude Hendrix (19-7), they were odds-on favorites to win the series.

'Twas not to be so.

Game number one, played in Chicago (at Comiskey Park rather than Cubs Park for the simple reason that Comiskey seated far more) on September 5, set the tone. In a Series that was to be dominated by pitching, the Bosox proved dominant. First-game starter Ruth topped Vaughn by the slimmest of margins. The Sox won, 1-0. Ruth allowed six hits; Vaughn, five. But one of those five was a scorching single off the bat of Stuffy that drove in secondbaseman Dave Shean (see page 36) with the contest's only tally in the fourth. (See sidebar on page 25 for juicy details.).

Game two belonged to one man. Lefty Tyler. The southpaw mainstay not only tossed a six-hitter; he drove in the game's winning runs with a two-run single into "centre"(as the word was then generally spelled) in the second inning as Chicago won, 3-1.

Game three was another low-scoring squeaker. The Sox tallied just two runs off Hippo Vaughn, back for his second shot at a win. The Cubs, though, managed only one tally off Sox submariner Carl Mays. Stuffy, after getting aboard with what was termed "a vicious clout" of a single, came around to score the winning run on a single by shortstop Everett Scott in the fourth.

Contest number four saw the Babe at his

NOTES FROM THE WORLD SERIES OF 1918

"The ninth inning saw the wise head of little Jack McInnis play an important part in the timely halt of another Cub rally. No player in the whole series has shown the baseball sense that the first-baseman of the Red Sox has displayed."

The New York Times of September 10, 1918, reporting on game four of the Series

"Stuffy called on every ounce of india rubber in his makeup, stuck one toe on the pillow and began to stretch. First he stretched only a few inches, then his body and arms stretched and stretched, half a foot at a time, until his hands seemed to reach half way down to the home plate. It was while he was in this marvelous condition of elasticity that he nipped the ball, and Merkle was out."

The New York Times of September 12, 1918, reporting on game six of the Series

"Next came to the bat Stuffy McInnis, the modest little graduate of the base-ball university of Connie Mack. Jack McInnis is a cool, cautious citizen in a pinch of this kind. If Manager Barrow had his choice, he could not have cho-

best again. Babe, the pitcher, that is. The big guy held the Mitchellmen to seven hits in a 3-2 Boston victory. Babe, the batter, did all right, too: his triple scored Stuffy, on base on a fielder's choice, with the winning run in the Sox fourth. The only negative: Ruth's record of 29⅔ innings of Series' shutout pitching came to a halt when the Cubs scored their two runs in the eighth.

The two clubs battled to another 1-0 thriller in game five. This time, though, it was the Sox who went scoreless as Hippo Vaughn was finally rewarded with a Series win. Worthy of note is that the game was delayed an hour when the players on both teams refused to take the field until they were assured they would receive what they'd been promised financially. (Ed. note: each Red Sox player eventually received $1,108.45; each Cub player, $671.00.).

The sixth and final confrontation between the two clubs saw Lefty Tyler and Carl Mays hook up in one last pitcher's duel. Lefty's efforts, however, were ruined when his right-fielder, Max Flack, muffed a routine fly in the third, allowing two Boston runners to score. That's all the Sox needed as Mays held the Cubs to a sole run. Stuffy was one for four at the plate, plus he played his usual sterling defense. (See sidebar this page for a closer look at one especially fine play.). The Red Sox were yet again World Champions. It's a statement they have not been able to make since.

From a Red Sox point of view, Stuffy's 1918 contributions are his most significant contributions. After all, one might ask, what could be

FIRST BASE

more important than winning the pennant and the World Series? And how many first-basemen have played on a Red Sox World Championship team in all the many years since Stuffy did it in that wartime summer of '18? (The answer, of course, is none.). But Stuffy's career was far from over after that glorious Championship season. The man from Gloucester played three more summers for the Bosox, batting .305 in 1919, .297 in 1920, and .307 in 1921. A holdout at the beginning of the 1921 season, Stuffy was traded to the Indians at the end of the season for George Burns (a .307 lifetime firstbaseman), Joe "Moon" Harris (a .317 lifetime firstbaseman/outfielder), and Elmer Smith (a .276 lifetime outfielder). After but one season in a Cleveland uniform – in which he hit .305 – Stuff was on the move again. In 1923 he ended up back in Boston. This time around, though, it was with the Braves. With the boys of Braves Field he played his last two seasons as a regular, batting a hearty .315 in 154 games in 1923 and .291 in 146 games in 1924. He also drove in 95 runs in 1923, no easy achievement when you consider how few runners the light-hitting seventh-place Braves had on base to knock in.

A holdout again in the spring of 1925, Stuffy was released to the Pirates. For the Bucs he appeared in 59 games in 1925, playing behind starting firstbaseman George Grantham. Still, though, Stuffy was a key factor in Pittsburgh's first pennant since 1909. He hit .368, best on a team that boasted Hazen "Kiki" Cuyler (.357) in right field, Max Carey (.343)

sen a better man than this same sawed-off lad from Gloucester.

Jim Vaughn's repertoire of curves responded beautifully to the twist of his fingers, and there was no fear in his heart as he speeded the ball over to little Jack. McInnis set himself, took a tremendous swing, and the ball hummed its way out to left field, while Shean started on a wild dash from second base.

Leslie Mann, Chicago's left fielder, raced over and checked the truant ball. Shean did not even stop to look, but tore around third base toward home as Mann picked up the ball and hurled it to Killefer. Shean may have had a badly injured finger, but there was nothing the matter with his feet, for he galloped home, taking the last few yards with a long, desperate slide, and beat the ball in by inches.

There was the ball game right there."

The New York Times of September 12, 1918, reporting on game six of the Series

"Boston is the luckiest baseball spot on earth, for it has never lost a world's series."

The New York Times of September 12, 1918, reporting on the sixth and final game of the Series in center, Grantham (.326) at first, Clyde "Pooch" Barnhart (.325) in left, fellow Massachusettsite Harold "Pie" Traynor (.320) at third, Earl Smith (.313) behind the plate, and Glenn "Buckshot" Wright (.308) at short. Stuffy's greatest contribution, however, came in the World Series, a Series that pitted the Pirates against the defending World Champion Washington Senators. The Bucs started slowly. They lost games one, three and four. With almost certain defeat staring him in the face, Pittsburgh manager Bill McKechnie played a hunch and started Stuffy in place of George Grantham in game five. The old vet acted as a steadying influence on the otherwise-youthful Pirate infield. Moreover, as an admirer named Joe Garland would later write in a Cape Ann publication called *North Shore*:

"The veteran knew every Senator like his brother." Stuffy had, after all, played 14 seasons in the Junior Circuit. As each Senator came to bat, "wise old Stuffy," as Garland called Stuff, would stroll over to Buc hurler Vic Aldridge and give advice on what to throw or not to throw. The combination of steadying and advising, again per Joe Garland, was "a magic that would never be forgotten by those who were there." Aldridge stopped the Senators, 6-3. Stuffy played first for the rest of the Series, a Series that saw "The Big Train," Walter Johnson, win two games and Washington outfielder Sam Rice make a catch that still ranks as one of the game's most controversial. And a Series that witnessed, for the first time in a best-of-seven tilt, a team that was down three games to one come back to win all

Stuffy played for five teams (not counting one at-bat with the Phillies in 1927) during his almost two-decade stay in the majors, and he batted over .300 in at least one season for each and every one of them. Here he is as he looked in a Cleveland uniform in 1922. For the Tribe that year he hit .305 in 142 games.

the marbles. Yep, the Bucs won. They took game six as Priate hurler Ray "Wiz" Kremer held Rice, Goose Goslin, Ossie Bluege, player/manager Bucky Harris, Joe Judge, and the rest of the Washington attack to six hits in a 3-2 Pirate win. The seventh and deciding game, played in Pittsburgh on a rain-soaked field, saw the Pirates wallop 15 hits (two by Stuffy) off a weary Walter Johnson to take World Championship honors.

With his heroics in the 1925 Series serving as a swan song, Stuffy finished out his playing career with the Pirates in 1926, hitting .299 in 47 games. Unfortunately, he was denied one last slice of World Series glory: the Cards, and not the Pirates, won the National League flag.

His active days behind him, Stuffy set his sights on a new career. Not surprisingly, it was also in baseball. First stop was managing the Phillies in 1927. That was almost certain to be a losing proposition: the Phils hadn't seen the light of the NL first division since 1917. They had, in fact, called last place their home in five of the previous nine seasons. Stuffy had been a marvelous ballplayer. But a magician he was not. The Phils, under his tutorage, posted a dismal 51-103 record, winding up in last place once again. From there Stuffy moved closer to home. Much closer. He managed the Salem Witches of the New England League in 1928. Then it was on to college ball. Stuffy coached at Norwich University (1929-1943), the Brooks School (1944-1946), Amherst (1947), and

Harvard (1948-1954). Ill health – he'd suffered from both Parkinson's disease and hardening of the arteries for many years – caused him to retire from the game he loved in 1954. A resident of Manchester, on Massachusetts' North Shore, for most of his life, the old first-sacker passed away at Cable Memorial Hospital in Ipswich on February 16, 1960.

P.S. There have been several attempts on the part of folks in and around Gloucester/Cape Ann to get Stuffy elected to the Hall of Fame. Lou Mandarini and Mel George, writing in *The Gloucester Daily Times*, have been especially active on Stuff's behalf. Alas, however, they have not had much success. Do I think Stuffy McInnis should adorn a plaque in Cooperstown? I sure do. Here's a player who is .308 lifetime over 19 seasons; ranks in the top 15 in six lifetime fielding categories; batted over .300 an even dozen times: rarely struck out; and played on six pennant winners and in five World Series. Legendary sportswriter Grantland Rice called Stuffy "a wargod of the diamond." My favorite sportswriter quote, though, comes from the typewriter of longtime Philadelphia scribe Wallace McCurley. Wrote Mr. McCurley: "Where is the old Athletic fan who does not remember how, on a dark day, all one could see of a bad throw to McInnis was a spurt of dust in front of the bag? That was all – the ball then would be nestled in his glove."

ULYSSES JOHN "TONY" LUPIEN,

shown here in a circa 1942 wire service photo, was born in Chelmsford, Massachusetts on April 23, 1917. A fine scholar as well as an athlete, he was a fancy-fielding firstbaseman and team captain for Harvard. From Harvard it was a short hop across the Charles to Fenway and a contract with the Red Sox. Replaced Jimmie Foxx as regular Sox first-baseman but never lived up to expectations. Played three years with Boston, 1940 and 1942-1943, then two with Phillies, 1944-1945, and one with White Sox, 1948. Top seasons were 1942, when hit .281, and 1944, when hit .283. Lifetime is .268 in 614 games.

ELBURT PRESTON "ELBIE" FLETCHER,

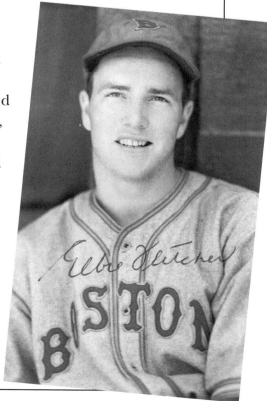

shown here in a circa 1937 photo, was born in Milton, Massachusetts on March 18, 1916 and died in Milton on March 9, 1994. Joined the Braves directly from Milton High in 1934; went on to play five seasons with Boston and seven with Pittsburgh. Was with Braves in 1935 when Babe Ruth was painfully ending his career. (Ed. note: this author had the distinct privilege of hearing Elbie speak at a 1993 Boston Braves Historical Association get-together. The firstsacker talked of how difficult it was to be on a team where one player – Babe – had one set of rules and the rest of the team had another). Best seasons were 1939, 1941, and 1942 when hit, respectively, .290, .288, and .289, and 1940, when drove in 104 runs. Lifetime is .271 in 1415 games.

FIRST BASE

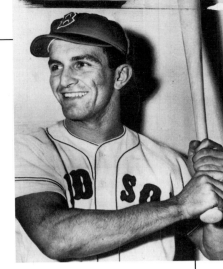

HARRY AGGANIS,
shown here smiling after he'd signed with Red Sox on November 28, 1952, was born in Lynn, Massachusetts on April 30, 1930 and died in Cambridge, Massachusetts on June 27, 1955. A marvelous all-around athlete, was a gifted southpaw quarterback for both Lynn Classical High School and Boston University. But excelled in baseball as well, and signed with Red Sox his senior year at BU. After one season with Louisville – in which he hit .281 with 23 homers and 108 RBIs – was called up. With Sox in 1954 hit .251 with eleven roundtrippers. Was hitting at a splendid .313 clip in 1955 when misfortune – in the form of a massive blood clot – struck. The man they called "The Golden Greek" died just as the season was rounding into form. Lifetime was .261 in 157 games.

FREDERICK CLAY "FRED" TENNEY,
looking rather roguish in *The Sporting News* of August 18, 1900, was born in Georgetown, Massachusetts on June 9, 1859 and died in Boston, Massachusetts on July 3, 1952. Starting as a lefthanded catcher out of Brown University, played 17 seasons in the majors, 1884-1909 and 1911, all but two of them with Boston's National League entry. Batted over .300 in seven of the 17; was player-manager in four of the 17. Is generally credited with invention of the firstbaseman's glove (originally called a "Tenney"). Lifetime is .295 in 1994 games.

GEORGE JOSEPH "CANDY" LaCHANCE,
shown here in a circa 1902 *Sporting Life* magazine illustration, was born in Waterbury, Connecticut on February 15, 1870 and died in Waterbury on August 18, 1932. Played twelve years in majors, 1893-1899 and 1901-1905, mostly with Brooklyn but also Baltimore, Cleveland, and Boston Americans (four seasons). With Boston appeared in first – 1903 – World Series. Batted over .300 five times. Lifetime is .280 in 1263 games. Was not called "Candy" because of his disposition. It was said to be bad.

Horace Hills "Hod" Ford

Hod Ford was a model of consistency for five big league teams, starting with the Braves in 1919 and finishing with the Braves, too, in 1933. He batted between .271 and .279 seven seasons in a row and eight seasons out of nine. Adept at either second or short, he was a slick gloveman who combined, during his Redleg days, with Hugh Critz to set the-then major league record of 128 double plays in a season in 1928. And, although not much of a power hitter, he set the-then Cincinnati mark for total-bases-in-a-game when he slugged out three doubles and a triple in a game against the Braves in May, 1930.

Our sole Connecticut starting-team representative, Horace Hills "Hod" Ford, was born in New Haven on July 23, 1897. He remained a New Havenite through elementary school, then moved with his family to Springfield, Massachusetts. After one year in "The City of Firsts," it was on to Somerville, Massachusetts, where Hod graduated from Somerville High in 1915. (Ed. note: Hod later moved to Winchester, Massachusetts, and it was there that he lived much of his adult life). At Somerville High, and various leagues in the area as well, he was a standout with both the glove and the bat. Teams for which he played

included the West Somerville Baptist Church, Falmouth Heights, the Queen Quality Shoe team, and both the Manchester-By-The-Sea and Marblehead nines. It is fair to say that all benefited from his presence in the line-up. Hod – or "Hoddy," as he was sometimes nicknamed – then starred at nearby Tufts.

While at Tufts, Hod was discovered by former big league catcher Jack Slattery and recommended to George Stallings, manager of the Braves. After signing Hod, the Braves, ironically, sent him back to his old stomping grounds, to New Haven, in the original Eastern League. Hod also appeared in ten games for the Braves in 1919, garnering six hits in 28 at-bats for a non-noteworthy .214 average. In 1920, he was with the big club all season long, playing behind Charlie Pick at second and the storied Rabbit Maranville at short, and improving to .241 in 88 games.

The season of 1921 saw a host of good things come Hod's way. He took over as the Braves' regular secondbaseman; he enjoyed his career-high number of at-bats, 555; hit a most respectful .279; led the league's second-sackers with an average-total-fielding-chances-per-game mark of 6.2…and he played on the closest thing he'd ever come to a pennant contender.

The Braves showed right off the bat, in 1921, that they were not to be the doormat they'd been in 1920 (and 1919 and 1918 and

SECOND BASE

Photo, June 1928. You'd be smiling, too, if your team were in first place – which the Reds were at the time, although they would wind up fifth – and you were on the way to leading the league in putouts, double plays, and fielding percentage.

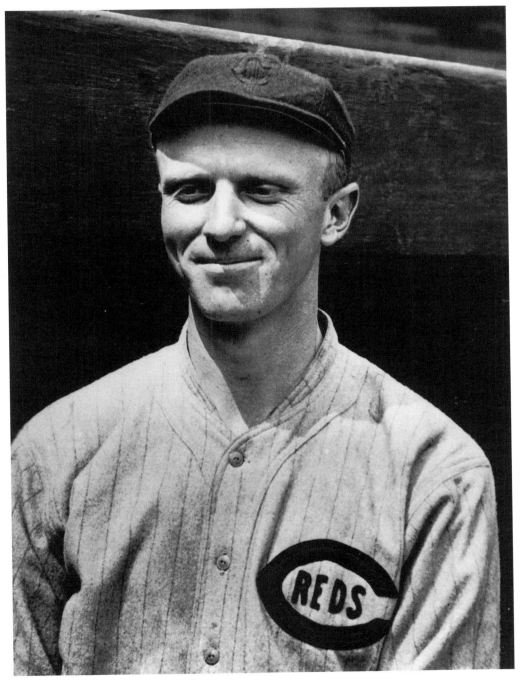

1917 and 1916). Their first five encounters of the season happened to be against the defending National League champs, the Dodgers (then usually called the Robins or Superbas), and the Braves happened to garner four of the five. The Brooklynites won game number one. Then they folded. In game two the Braves took it, 11-4, manhandling three Superba hurlers "in a manner that should," reported *The New York Times*, "be brought to the attention of the Prevention of Cruelty to Aspiring Athletes." The third contest went ten innings, with the Braves emerging victorious, 6-5, as Hod drove in the winning run by drawing a bases-loaded walk. Game four saw yet another Brave win, as Brooklyn lost, 7-1, and, again per the witty words of *The Times*, "did not even have the satisfaction of having put up a strong battle." The two teams' final match once more went to the Beaneaters (an old name for the Braves then still in use), 4-2. Yet again *The Times*: "For the fourth time in succession the Boston Braves punched the Brooklyn Robins on the nose and got away with it."

Hod played in every inning of all five games, going just three for 15 at the plate, but holding down his post like glue, and making it clear to new skipper Fred Mitchell (see page 134) that Hod Ford was the man for the team's second base job.

The Braves of 1921 were not the Miracle Braves of 1914. But they were good. And they were consistent: lodging themselves in third and remaining there for most of the season. Better-known players on the team included

rightfielder (and later long-time manager) Billy Southworth, who batted .308; veteran catcher Hank Gowdy, who batted .299; and pitcher Joe Oeschger, who was 20-14 in his best-ever season on the hill.

In late June there emerged a rumor that showman George M. Cohan wanted to purchase a major league team. Specifically, that he wanted to purchase the Braves. George M., however, quickly squashed that story. Yes, admitted the man who wrote *Give My Regards to Broadway*, he wanted to buy a team. But, no, it wasn't the Braves.

The season of 1921 also saw much conjecture that the ball being used had been made more lively. (Ed. note: sound familiar?). Julian Curtiss, president of A.G. Spalding & Bros., makers of the ball used in the National League, however, vigorously denied it. "Permit me to state most emphatically that there has been no changes made in the manufacture of this ball," said he.

Those matters under control, Hod and the Braves rolled along in third place. As one sportswriter put it: "The Braves (and Cardinals) have made spurts, only to subside when the heights loomed up."

September saw the Braves subside out of third. On September 1 the team was held to five hits (two of them by Hod), losing to the Phils, 1-0, while the Cards were sweeping a doubleheader from the Pirates, 10-4 and 8-0, thereby taking over the third spot. John McGraw and his Giants, meanwhile, claimed the top rung from the Pirates, and went on to win the pennant, setting up the first of a long line – some would say far too long a line – of World Series in which both teams were New York teams.

For the Braves, 1921, at 79-74, turned out to be their strongest season in the 17-year span from 1916 to 1933 (when Wally Berger's 27 home runs and 106 RBIs spearheaded the Braves to 83-71). For Hod, 1921 was an excellent year. He was at the top of his superlative defense, and he proved he was no slouch with the stick, either. In fact, his .279 was twelve points higher than that of Johnny Rawlings, who held down second for the pennant-winning Giants. (Although Hod did finish a notch or two behind the man at second for the Cards, the man with the distinctive first name, Rogers Hornsby. "The Rajah" slammed out a major-league leading .397 that summer of 1921.).

Hod Ford labored for ten additional full seasons in the majors, all in the National League, and all for less-than-fully-successful teams. If it wasn't the Braves (1922-1923), it was the Phillies (1924), or the Dodgers (part of 1925: he played for Minneapolis that season, too), or the Reds (1926-1931). Whatever the club, it would always be mired in the second division, and Hod would always bat in the .270's. Or almost always: he slipped to .241 in 1928 and .231 in 1930. The sole variable was the position the man from New Haven/ Somerville/Winchester would play. Sometimes it was second. Sometimes it was short. Whichever, he always played it well. One of his

finest games came, ironically, as he was winding down his career in 1930. Hod batted but .231 in 132 games for the Reds that year. And *that* year was the Year of the Hitter. Hack Wilson blasted 56 homers and drove in an amazing 190 runs. Memphis Bill Terry hit .401, the last National Leaguer to achieve the coveted .400 mark. Every player in the league with 400 or more at-bats, in fact, hit over .250. Except for one player. And that one player was Hod. Yet on May 5 he, too, joined in the hit parade. In a game against his former team, the Braves, Hod knocked out three doubles and a triple, scoring twice and driving in four. His total base count for the game added up to nine, good enough to be the then-Cincinnati all-time high.

Perhaps bolstered by his batting rampage against the Braves or perhaps because he realized his playing time was running short, Hod became a holdout going into the season of 1931. He notified Redleg management that he was working out at his alma mater, Tufts, but had no intention of reporting to the Reds' training camp in Tampa unless offered a more lucrative contract. He had been asked to take a pay cut of 40% and he wasn't any too happy about it. A compromise was eventually reached and Hod was on hand for – and played in – the Reds' opener. He would, however, appear in but 83 more games that season, losing his job at second to Tony Cuccinello and at short to West Springfield, Massachusetts' native son, Leo Durocher. The reason: youth. The road to success, declared Reds' management, lay with

Hod in a posed photo from 1930. In that year, in which it seemed as if everybody and his brother in the league turned into a slugger, Hod batted a dismal .231. Still, though, in a game against his former teammates, the Braves, on May 5 the normally mild-mannered infielder slammed out three doubles and a triple to set the-then Cincinnati mark for total bases in a single game. It was an afternoon he would long remember.

SECOND BASE

Baseball card companies have not always been sacrosanct with respect to the photos they used on their cards. If the shot of Hod on the 1933 Big League shown here appears to be remarkably similar to the photo on the facing page, that's because – with the exception of background alterations – it is. Nineteen-thirty-three was Hod's last season in a major league uniform. Back with the Braves, he would get into just five games, getting one hit in 15 trips to the plate for an anemic .067 mark.

younger players. Cuccinello was 23; Leo, 25; Hod, 33.

On January 26, 1932, Hod was sold to the Cardinals. The papers called it St. Louis "pennant insurance:" that Hod "will always be ready to hop into action and do some fancy fielding." It was to be, however, very short-lived pennant insurance. Hod played in exactly one game for the Cards before moving on to the Braves. For his old team he batted .274 in 40 games, then joined Toronto in the International League for 41 more. Toss in five games – and an .067 batting average – for the Braves in 1933 and you have the finale to Hod's baseball career.

After his playing days, Hod Ford retired back to Winchester where he owned and operated a successful confectionery and restaurant. He died in Winchester on January 29, 1977.

DAVID WILLIAM "DAVE" SHEAN, portrayed below on a 1911 American Beauty Cigarettes' card, was born in Ware, Massachusetts on May 23, 1878 and died in Boston, Massachusetts on May 22, 1963. Played for Athletics, Phillies, Braves (called "Rustlers" in 1911), Cubs, Reds, and Red Sox in nine-year major league career. Best offensive year was 1918 when batted .264 with 16 doubles for Red Sox. With Sox he played in all six games of the 1918 World Series – at age 40 – hitting .211 with two runs scored in Sox win over Cubs. Lifetime is .228 in 630 games.

ALBERT SAYLES "HOBE" FERRIS, shown above in a circa 1904 photo, was born in Providence, Rhode Island on December 7, 1877 and died in Detroit, Michigan on March 18, 1938. Was an adroit fielder with punch in his bat. Hit eight home runs in 1902 (tied for sixth best in AL) and nine in 1903 (third best in AL). Played first seven of his nine major league seasons, 1901-1909, with Pilgrims/Puritans/Somersets/Red Sox); last two with St. Louis Browns. Was hero of eighth and deciding game of first World Series, 1903, when drove in all three runs in Boston victory, 3-0, over Pittsburgh. Lifetime is .239 in 1286 games.

AMBROSE MOSES "AMBY" McCONNELL,

portrayed here on a 1911 "Turkey Red" card, was born in North Pownal, Vermont on April 29, 1883 and died in Utica, New York on May 20, 1942. Was Red Sox starting secondbaseman in 1908 and 1909; then traded with Harry Lord to White Sox in August 1910. Best seasons in four-year major league career, 1908-1911, were 1911, when hit .280 in 104 games for Chisox, and 1908, when hit .279 in 140 games for Bosox. Was one of the three Vermont natives – Larry Gardner and Ray Collins being the others – on Red Sox in 1909-1910. With Bosox was part of Red Sox "Speed Boys," stealing 57 bases in the two years he was a regular. Lifetime is .264 in 409 games.

McCONNELL BOSTON AMER.

FRED EDWARD "FREDDIE" MAGUIRE

– no photo available – was born in Roxbury, Massachusetts on May 10, 1899 and died in Brighton, Massachusetts on November 3, 1961. The slender infielder – he stood 5'11"/weighed but 155 pounds - played a few games for Giants in 1922-1923, then bounced around minors until 1928 when landed with the Cubs. With Cubbies enjoyed his best season, 1928, batting .279 in 140 games. At season's end, in November, was traded to Braves with four other players and $200,000 for Rogers Hornsby. Was regular secondbaseman for Braves, 1929-1931. Lifetime is .257 in 618 games.

Frederick Alfred "Freddy" Parent

Our starting shortstop was one of the heroes of the first modern (i.e. played between the winners of the American and National Leagues) World Series, in 1903, a scrappy little guy who could hit and field and was at the core of the Red Sox's earliest successes. Born in Biddeford, Maine, he would go on to become synonymous with baseball in nearby Sanford, Maine.

Born in Biddeford, Maine on November 25, 1875, Freddy Parent was short on schooling, long on work ethic. Early in life he went to work in a Sanford textile mill. There he toiled at a loom from 7:00 AM to 6:00 PM Monday through Friday.

Come Saturday, though, he was out playing baseball every day the weather would permit. Finally, in 1898, he decided to follow his heart and give ballplaying a full-time shot: he signed on with New Haven in the Connecticut League. He did well enough to get a brief (two games at second) shot with the St. Louis Cardinals in mid-July of 1899, before being returned to New Haven. In 1900 he moved up to Providence in the International League, where he batted leadoff and was a mainstay both offensively and defensively. He came up to the major leagues to stay, with the Boston entry in the brand-new American League, in 1901.

In his first season in Boston, Freddy showed that, though he stood but 5' 5½" tall and weighed only 148 pounds, he could play with the best of them. In 138 games he poked a solid .306, scoring 87 runs and driving in 59 more, as Boston finished second only to Chicago. The following year, 1902, Freddy led the league both in times at bat (567) and number of assists (496), while batting a creditable .275.

It is the season of 1903, however, that warrants our longest look. For one thing, it was our shortstop's most significant season. Secondly, it was the year of the very first World Series (with Freddy and crew there to take home all the honors). Third, whether we like it or not, 1903 was the year that the most dominant team in sports history, the New York Yankees, was "born."

Let's start with number three. The American League was going into its third summer of existence in 1903. It was doing well by all accounts. One important thing it lacked, however, was a presence in the nation's largest city, New York City. But league prexy Ban Johnson was about to rectify that situation. He lined up a pair of New York bigwigs who put up $18,000, purchased the league's Baltimore franchise, and moved it to New York. Contrary to what has been written repeatedly, the new team was not nicknamed the "Highlanders." It was called the "Greater New Yorks." And, per the pages of *The New York Times* anyway, the team kept the Greater New York moniker – as

SHORTSTOP

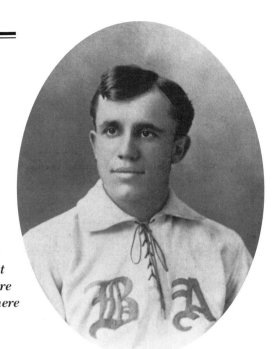

Freddy Parent, shown here in a circa 1903 photo, was the Boston American's very first shortstop. Long before there was Nomar there was Freddy.

unbedazzling as it was – through April of 1907. Then they took on the name we all know: the "Yankees." There's no doubt that, along the way, the club was also called the "Highlanders" (as well as the "Hilltoppers," after Hilltop Park, their home grounds), but it appears to have been on a more or less here-and-there basis.

The Bostons, meanwhile, began 1903 on the slow side. Their opener was a separate-admission twinbill in Boston on Patriot's Day, April 20, versus Philadelphia. A hefty crowd of 8,876 turned out for the first game, played in the morning. Boston won that one, 9-4. They lost the second, however, as over 11,000 looked on as Philadelphia scored ten runs to Boston's seven. The team then went 7-7 and was nestled in fifth place in the eight-team loop when they first encountered the Greater New Yorks. It was the world première match-up between the team that would become the Red Sox and the team that would become the Yankees. The

game was played at Boston's Huntington Avenue Grounds on May 7. Included here, in its entirety, is *The New York Times'* write-up of that contest – as relayed to New York by *The Times'* Boston correspondent – because (A) the game was definitely an historic event in its own way, and (B) because I find it both fun and fascinating to read all these many decades later. So here goes:

The New York American League team lost the first game of a series with the Bostons to-day by a score of 6-2. Batting when hits counted was the deciding element in a game which was interesting from start to finish. Until the seventh inning was reached clever fielding by the visitors had kept the Boston score down to 3 runs. In that inning, however, the Bostons scored three times, and the result of the contest thereafter was never in doubt. While the home team only scored 6 tallies, 5 of them were earned.

A spectacular running catch by Fultz, the centre fielder of the New Yorks, was the fielding feature. With the exception of Dineen every man on the home team made at least one hit. Ferris's single safe drive netted four bases, while Stahl, whose batting was the feature of Boston's work, had two three-base drives and a single to his credit.

To Dineen, however, belongs the greatest share of credit for the victory. He was almost invincible, and the six hits made by the New Yorks were scattered over almost as many innings. Wiltse, on the other hand, was batted even more freely than the score would indicate.

Herman Long, who made his first appearance here in a foreign uniform, was pre-sented with a diamond pin.

Over 100 years later the words written that May day still read relatively well. We spell "to-day" and "centre field" differently now. And we know that "Dineen" was really "Dinneen" ("Big Bill" Dinneen, star Boston moundsman). We call a "three-base drive" a triple. We probably wouldn't use the term "in a foreign uniform" to indicate a player now on another team. Then there's "Ferris's single safe drive netted four bases." It takes a moment or so to figure that one out. Nowadays we'd be more apt to say something like "Ferris had only one hit but it was a homer." Anyway you word things, though, May 7, 1903 was a splendid day for the Boston Americans. And for Freddy Parent.

Circa 1904 postcard view

When Boston proved victorious in the 1903 World Series, Freddy took his share of the loot – it totaled to $1,182.00 – and bought this house in Sanford. He would live there most of the rest of his long life.

FRED PARENT AND HIS NEW RESIDENCE, SANFORD, ME.

SHORTSTOP

Batting fifth in the line-up, as he would all season long, the shortstop contributed a double and a single and scored a run.

Game two between the clubs, played on May 8, was the least interesting of the bunch. With North Adams, Massachusetts' native (and future Hall of Famer) Jack Chesbro holding Boston to six hits, the Greater New Yorks won, 6-1. Freddy went hitless. The game's write-up was on the lackluster side, too. Come the third and last game, however, and we have ourselves a memorable event once more. I am going to, in fact, allow *The Times*' Boston correspondent to again tell you about it. Headlined "Unruly New York Players Ordered Out of the Game and Boston Won," the article read:

> A decision by Umpire Caruthers in the fifth inning of to-day's baseball game was undoubtedly the cause of the defeat of the Greater New Yorks. Up to that time Tannehill had been pitching balls which the Bostonians could not hit, and had the game in hand. When Stahl was at bat in the fifth Caruthers instead of calling the third strike called a ball and Stahl promptly drove the (next) ball for two bases, scoring Dougherty and advancing Gibson to third. The visiting players flocked to the plate in protest and the argument became so warm that Williams assaulted the umpire. Tannehill also lost control of his tongue to such an extent that Caruthers sent him as well as Williams off the field. After this Howell went into pitch, and he was pounded right and left to the delight of the great crowd that cheered itself hoarse.

"Tannehill" was stellar hurler Jesse Tannehill, who would wear a Boston American uniform the next season (and for whom he would be a 20-game winner in both 1904 and 1905). The Boston nine chalked up 17 hits that afternoon, with Freddy having three of them; two singles and a "three-base drive." The winning moundsman in the 12-5 rout was none other than Cy Young, who would go on to a 28-9 season for the Bostons.

So the teams that would become arch rivals were off and running. At each other's throats. That was ok. And with Boston taking two of three. That was ok, too.

Boston went on, of course, to win the 1903 American League flag, with Philadelphia, Cleveland, and New York following. Freddy was a major factor in the Bostons' success. Some statistics: the Pride of Sanford led all American League shortstops with a .304 batting average, stole 24 bases, scored 83 runs, and knocked in 80. His 80 RBIs were exceeded on the club by only rightfielder Buck Freeman's league-leading 104. His .304 average was bettered on the club by only leftfielder Patsy Dougherty's third-best-in-the-league mark of .331.

But Freddy was more than statistics. In his book THE BOSTON RED SOX (New York City: G.P. Putnam's Sons, 1947), Frederick Lieb wrote of him: "Parent was built close to the ground...but he had surprising dexterity in getting over the ground, took the spikes of the toughest base runners, was a fast runner himself and a dangerous hitter in the clutch." Garry Herrmann, president of the Cincinnati

Reds, went considerably further in lavishing praise: in 1904 he called Freddy Parent the best shortstop in the major leagues.

But, back to 1903. Barney Dreyfuss, owner of the National League champs, the Pirates, was so confident that he could put the upstart "Junior Circuit" in its place that he challenged the Bostons to a best-of-nine series. Henry J. Killilea, the Pilgrims' prexy, accepted. The match was on!

At the outset of the contest it certainly appeared as if Dreyfuss' prediction would prove correct. Game number one, played in Boston on October 1, saw Pittsburgh score four times in the first inning and go on to win handily, 7-3. Freddy accounted for two – one of which was a triple – of the Pilgrims' total of six hits, and scored one of the team's three runs. In game two the Bostons bounced back, with Big Bill Dinneen shutting down the Bucs, 3-0. The third game was pretty much a repeat of the first: Pirate hurler Charles "Deacon" Phillippe (who would pitch five games in the Series) bested Boston's ace, Cy Young, with Pittsburgh winning, 4-2. In game four, with two days of rain giving his arm some rest, the Deacon came back…and won again, this time by a score of 5-4. The Pirates now had a rather commanding 3-1 lead in games. Game five, however, saw a turnaround. The Bostons belted the Bucs, amassing 14 hits in an 11-2 romp. Freddy contributed two of the 14 hits and scored a run. Game number six was more of the same. Freddy managed to get hit by a pitch in one at bat and he socked a triple in another

and scored two runs (plus his fielding was noted as a feature of the game in the media accounts of the game) as the Pilgrims again came out on top, 6-3. The seventh game saw an overflow crowd of 17,308 jam its way into the Pirates' Exposition Park. With fans taking over much of the outfield it was agreed that any ball hit into the crowd would be a ground-rule triple. The result was that there was an almost unheard of total of seven triples in the game, with Freddy's bat accounting for one of them. He also chipped in with a single, two runs scored, and fielding that the press again applauded. That gave the Bostons the advantage…plus play shifted back to their home park, the Huntington Avenue Grounds. Two days of rain postponed the excitement…and again allowed Deacon Phillippe enough rest to take the mound one more time. He pitched well, too. But not well enough. Big Bill Dinneen did better, holding the Bucs to four hits (it would have been five but Freddy made a great grab of a liner off the bat of Fred Clarke). To the "almost frenzied delight," as worded by *The Times*, of 17,000 rooters, the home team won, 3-0. It was October 13, 1903. And the Bostons were the world's first World Champions!

What's especially noteworthy – from a Series wrap-up point of view – is how one shortstop outplayed the other all during the Series. And the one that did the outplaying was the one from Maine. It may well, in fact, have been the difference in the Series' outcome. At the bat Freddy clearly outshone his counterpart, the one and only Honus Wagner. Wagner, considered by most to be the greatest shortstop in baseball history, had batted .355 during the regular season, winning the second of his record eight batting championships. In the Series, however, he slumped to .222, with but one extra base hit (a double), two runs scored, and three runs batted in. He struck out four times. Freddy, meanwhile, chimed in with a .281 average, had three extra base hits (all triples), scored eight runs, and knocked in three. He struck out but once. In the field, too, Freddy shone. Accounts of the day make mention of his fielding in several instances. Little is said about the play of "The Flying Dutchman."

In terms of cold, hard statistics, the box scores show that Freddy made 17 putouts to Honus' ten; had slightly more assists, 29 vs. 27; and, most telling, that Honus made five errors to Freddy's two. Eight games, of course, do not a career make, and no one is about to suggest that Honus Wagner's plaque in Cooperstown be replaced with Freddy's. Still, for half a month in an autumn classic of long ago, one Frederick Alfred Parent was clearly king of the shortstop hill.

In 1904, the boys from Boston took the league flag again. Surprisingly, they did it without a single .300 hitter in the lineup. Freddy's .291 was the second highest on the team,

Greatly enlarged (the original is 1⅜″ x 2½″) Hassan Cigarettes' baseball card, 1911

WHEN THE RED SOX BECAME THE RED SOX

Although he played for the White Sox from 1908 until 1911, Freddy is best known for his work with the Red Sox. In fact it was while he was with them, in 1907, that the Red Sox became the Red Sox. Up until then the team had been known, variously, as the Somersets, the Puritans, and the Pilgrims. When club owner John I. Taylor got wind, in the spring of 1907, that the Boston entry in the National League was going to abandon their red stockings, he immediately ordered red hose for his team...and christened them the "Red Sox."

exceeded only by centerfielder Chick Stahl's .295. With moundsmen the likes of Cy Young (26-16, with an ERA of 1.97), Bill Dinneen (23-14, with a 2.20 ERA), and Jesse Tannehill (21-11, with an ERA of 2.04), though, who needed much hitting? Actually the race for the pennant was a seesaw battle with the Greater New Yorks right down to the very wire. The title, in fact, was not decided until a doubleheader played in New York on October 10. If they won either game, the Pilgrims were champions. If they lost both, however, the New Yorkers would

have it. In the little park, with a seating capacity of 12,000, over 28,000 enthusiasts somehow wedged their way in. They saw a humdinger. With the score deadlocked at 2-2 in the top of the ninth, New York pitcher Jack Chesbro (who was going for his 42nd win of the season!) allowed leadoff batter Lou Criger to reach first via an infield hit. Pitcher Bill Dinneen sacrificed Criger to second. The Boston catcher then went to third on an out by Kip Selbach. That brought Freddy to the plate. Chesbro reared back with his best pitch – the

FREDDY KNEW WHAT THE BABE COULD DO

Freddy was always proud of his role in the discovery of Babe Ruth. The man from Maine was playing for Baltimore when the Babe joined the Orioles, then a minor league team, as a left-handed pitcher in the spring of 1914. Later that same season Red Sox manager Bill Carrigan wanted to know about Ruth and teammate Ernie Shore. Freddy's advice: "If you can get those two you'll win the pennant." The rest is history.

Babe Ruth! Babe Ruth! (We Know What He Can Do) sheet music, 1928

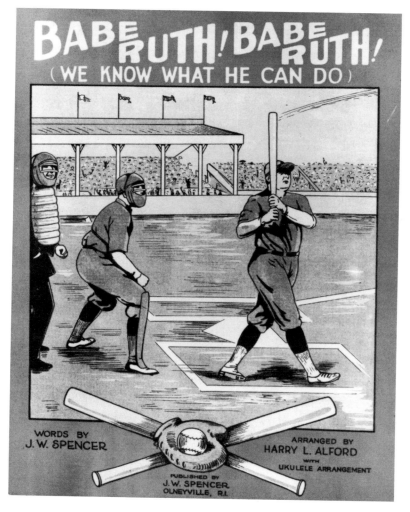

spitter, then still legal – but it sailed out of his hand and over Freddy's head for a wild pitch. In trotted Lou Criger with the run that won the pennant.

There would be no World Series that year, however. John T. Brush, owner of the National League-winning Giants (and a man with a zealous hatred of the American League: he referred to the New York Americans as the "Invaders"), simply refused to allow his team to play. His club was, as he phrased it, "content to rest on its laurels."

Those pennant-winning years of 1903 and 1904 were Freddy's banner seasons. He played three additional years for Boston, but his bat had lost some of its sting. He dropped to .234 in 1905, rose a notch to .235 in 1906 (the infamous year when both Boston teams finished dead last), improved to .276 in 1907. It was in this latter year that Freddy began to do some outfielding as well as playing shortstop.

In April of 1908, Freddy was peddled to the White Sox for an undisclosed amount of cash. There were those who thought that he'd slowed down to the point where, at age 32, his playing days were numbered; that playing just shy of 1,000 games in his seven years with Boston had taken its toll. Freddy did his best to prove the critics wrong. His time with the White Sox, however, was a disappointment to him. In 1908 he batted but .207 in 119 games, all at shortstop. By splitting duties between the infield and the outfield in 1909 he had his last good season: a .261 mark – with a career high total of 32 stolen bases – in 136 games. In 1910

he plummeted to .178, mostly as a part-time outfielder. He was released by the Sox after three games in 1911.

After a very full dozen years in the bigs, Freddy drifted on back to the minors. There was no way he was ready to quit yet. He played short or second – and coached some, too – for Jack Dunn's International League Baltimore Orioles from 1911 through 1914. That the old pro could still play was evidenced by his .306 batting average in 149 games in 1912. From 1915 to 1917 Freddy played and managed semi-pro ball for the (Sanford, Maine) Goodall Textiles, returning to organized ball as player-manager for Springfield in the Eastern League in 1918 and, closer to home, manager of the Lewiston Red Sox in the New England League in 1919. From 1922 through 1925 Freddy was head baseball coach at Colby. He was then junior varsity coach at Harvard from 1926 until 1928. After that it was back to Maine for good…where he played some and coached a lot right up through the 1940s. He also owned and operated a gas station. But most of all, Freddy Parent was a rabid supporter of Little League and American Legion ball. He once, in fact, even gave his old playing days' glove to the most valuable player on one of the local Little League squads.

Mr. World Series Shortstop of 1903 died in a Sanford nursing home on November 2, 1972. He was just three weeks short of his ninety-seventh birthday.

JOHN JOSEPH "JACK" BARRY

Shown here in a circa 1912 photograph, was born in Meriden, Connecticut on April 26, 1887 and died in Shrewbsury, Massachusetts on April 23, 1961. A standout at Holy Cross, he was signed by Connie Mack; went on to be a key ingredient in Mack's famed $100,000 Athletics' infield. Was starting shortstop on Athletics' teams that won AL flag in 1910, 1911, 1913, and 1914. Batted .368 with four doubles in 1911 Series and .300 with three doubles in 1913 Series, both won by A's. Sold to Red Sox for $8,000 on July 2, 1915; played with Sox – as secondbaseman – through 1919. Appeared in his fifth Series, 1915, as Sox took Phillies, four games to one. Player-managed the Red Sox to a 90-62 second-place record in 1917. Traded back to A's in June 1919 but refused to report, retiring instead. Lifetime is .243 in 1222 games.

HAROLD CHANDLER "HAL" JANVRIN, pictured here ready to scoop up a hot one circa 1914, was born in Haverhill, Massachusetts on August 27, 1892 and died in Boston on March 2, 1962. A good utility infielder with a weak bat, he joined the Red Sox as a nineteen-year old in 1911 and played six seasons with them. Later played for Senators, Cardinals, and Dodgers in ten-year major league career that stretched through 1922. Appeared in all five games of 1916 World Series, rapping out three doubles to help Bosox beat Brooklyn. Lifetime is .232 in 756 games.

WILLIAM LORENZ "LARRY" KOPF – no photo available – was born in Bristol, Connecticut on November 3, 1890 and died in Anderson Township, Ohio on October 15, 1986. He was a sure and steady shortstop, starting with Cleveland, 1913, and finishing with Braves, 1921-1922. In between came the Athletics, 1914-1915, and the Reds, 1916-1917 and 1919-1921. Best year was 1919 when hit .270 with 18 stolen bases to help Reds win both NL flag and World Series against tainted White Sox. His triple with two on was key hit in Series game two, won by Reds, 4-2. Second best year was 1922 when hit .266 in 126 games for Braves. Younger brother Walter Henry "Wally" Kopf (born Stonington, Connecticut, July 10, 1899/died April 30, 1979 in Cincinnati, Ohio) appeared in two games at third for Giants in 1921. Larry's lifetime is .249 in 850 games.

William Lawrence "Larry" Gardner

Vermonter Larry Gardner was a star thirdbaseman for the Bosox, A's, and Indians. He hit .315 in 1912 and .308 in 1916 and played in as many Red Sox World Series as Johnny Pesky, Rico Petrocelli, Frank Malzone, and Butch Hobson combined. Known as "The Diving Thirdbaseman," Larry Gardner was a mean man with the glove, too, possessing an uncanny ability to spear ground balls and having an arm that one sportswriter called "a cannon with precision."

"College boys" were not readily accepted into the rough and tumble world of early 20th century baseball. There were exceptions, of course, and many of these exceptions seemed to play for the Boston Americans. Early collegians who went on to play for Boston included topnotch outfielders Harry Hooper and Duffy Lewis, firstbaseman/manager Jake Stahl, thirdbaseman/manager Jimmy Collins, secondbaseman Amby McConnell, catcher/manager Bill Carrigan, thirdbaseman Harry Lord, pitcher Ray Collins, and thirdbaseman Larry Gardner. The last three were intertwined. Gardner replaced Lord at third after the 1910 season. Gardner and Collins had been teammates at the University of Vermont.

Born in Enosburg Falls, a smallish community in the northwestern part of Vermont, on May 13, 1886, Larry Gardner was a smart kid who was also a fine athlete. And with each succeeding year he became a finer athlete. Larry entered the University of Vermont in the autumn of 1905 and almost immediately advanced to star status on the diamond. He played such a strong game both offensively and defensively that, even years later in 1986, the University of Vermont's *Vermont* (now known as *Vermont Quarterly*) would recall Larry as "a .400 hitter with a penchant for making spectacular plays." He captained the team in 1908. That same year he was approached by the Red Sox, among other teams, and elected to go pro. Larry chose the Sox because they were the "home team."

The youngster – he was but 22 – sat on the Bosox bench for a handful of games and was then loaned to Lynn in the New England League. With Lynn, Larry showed what was to come by holding down a tight shortstop and batting .305 in 61 games. The Sox were convinced; they brought Larry up for the 1909 season. Not that they allowed him any appreciable playing time. The star-to-be saw action in 19 games; collected splinters in the other 132. Two breaks caused Larry's status to change from benchwarmer to starter. Break number one – for Larry, anyway – was secondbaseman and fellow Vermont-native Amby McConnell's taking ill in the spring of 1910. Larry grabbed his glove and took over. The man from

THIRD BASE

Enosburg Falls ended up playing in 113 games, all at second, while batting an impressive .283. Break number two was management's disenchantment with starting thirdbaseman Harry Lord. The Porter, Maine native was considered by at least some of the team's hierarchy to be, according to Frederick G. Lieb in his classic 1947 book, THE BOSTON RED SOX, guilty of sulking, of overplaying injuries, and of being "money mad." The result was that Lord (and Amby McConnell) was traded to the White Sox on August 9. The next season, 1911, saw Larry play 62 games at second and 72 at third. He batted .285, hit a career-high four homers, and

"College boys" were few and far between in the early years of 20th century baseball. But Larry Gardner was one of them, going from stardom at the University of Vermont to stardom for the Bosox.

Circa 1910 photograph

49

ON MAKING FRIENDS

"Too much of this sort of thing is more than a-plenty. All season long the Yankees have submitted meekly to being trimmed by the Boston Red Sox and have never whimpered. But along came Boston yesterday, and, not satisfied with a daily victory, imposed on good nature and grabbed two in one afternoon. That's no way to make friends."

The New York Times, June 23, 1912, on the occasion of a twinbill sweep of the Yankees by the Red Sox after the Sox had won all five previous outings between the two clubs that season as well.

scored 80 runs. The Sox finished the year with a 78-75 mark, good for only fifth. But they were bubbling.

The year of 1912, Larry Gardner's first full season holding down the hot corner for the Bosox, was supposed to be a Philadelphia year. Connie Mack's marauders had, after all, been World Champs in both 1910 and 1911 and the team's fabled $100,000 infield was still very much intact, as was the superb pitching staff anchored by Colby Jack Coombs, Eddie Plank, and Chief Bender. In fact, Connie was known to say that the 1912 Athletics were his best team ever.

But the "best evers" didn't win that year. They were, as it turned out, to finish but third in the AL. Second went to the surprising Washington Senators. And first was the Red Sox. The team started right off being first, too.

Of course it helped that they began the season against the then-hapless New York Yankees. The Sox took their first three – all in New York at old Hilltop Park – by scores of 5-3, 5-2, and 8-4. Wrote *The New York Times* after Sox victory number one on April 11: "A ninth-inning batting rally by the Boston Red Sox furnished the only discordant note in an otherwise successful inaugural of the baseball season on the Hilltop yesterday afternoon, the Yankees losing their 1912 opener to the Beantown warriors by the score of 5-3." Larry was 0 for 2 with a walk in game one; one for four, a double, with a run scored in number two; and one for five in number three. His hit in the third contest was described as "a scorcher." Three in a row against the Yankees. That's fun.

As if to prove their three-in-a-row was no fluke, Boston manager – and firstbaseman –

THIRD BASE

Jake Stahl then led his charges into Philadelphia and took the favored Athletics, 9-2. Larry was two for four, and turned two line drives into double plays as well.

A very special day, indeed, was April 20. After several rainouts, the Bostonians finally had the chance to unveil their brand new and magnificent $350,000 stadium. Its name was Fenway Park. Over 27,000 folks, the largest baseball crowd ever to be seen in Boston until then, turned out to cheer on the home team. What a game they saw! At one point the New Yorkers had a 5-1 lead, but the home team came charging back with three in the fourth, and single tallies in the sixth, seventh, and the eleventh. The one in the eleventh did it. Final score: Boston, 7; New York, 6. Larry played a flawless third and was two for six at the plate.

For much of the season manager Jake Stahl and his team fought it out with the White Sox and the Senators. A 17-game win streak by the Nats in June didn't hurt their cause. President Bill Taft – *big* Bill Taft: he weighed in at a hefty 332 pounds – was even on hand for what was to

Here's Walter Johnson as he appeared on a 1912 Hassan Cork Tip Cigarettes card. Even the Big Train didn't win them all.

THE BIG TRAIN VS. SMOKY JOE

A very definite BIG game of 1912 was the much-heralded contest of September 6 when the second-place Senators squared off against the number one Red Sox. On the hill for the Senators: "The Big Train," Walter Johnson. On the hill for the Sox: Smoky Joe Wood. Johnson had earlier that season won sixteen games in a row…was on his way to a 32-12 mark. Smoky Joe was at fourteen in a row…on his way to a 34-5 mark. The game, played before 20,000 screaming fans at Fenway, was a tight one. A pitcher's duel par excellence. The Big Train was good…Smoky just a little better. Final score: Boston, 1 – Washington, 0.

turn out to be the Senator's number 17, on June 18. Mr. Taft threw out the first ball before repairing with Mrs. Taft to a pair of front row – presumably *big* front row – box seats.

Another special game – even though it was a losing one – was a contest against Cleveland on June 4. It was the 10th anniversary of Napoleon Lajoie with the Indians...and it was "Lajoie's Day" at the Indians' old League Park. The "Woonsocket Wonder" – arguably the finest ballplayer ever to come out of New England – was presented with 1,000 silver dollars, from the fans, and $125.00 in gold, a gift from his teammates. Nappy then went and banged out a double, single, and sacrifice fly in a 5-1 Cleveland win.

In a season he would undoubtedly treasure forever, Larry Gardner enjoyed many a memorable game. Some that stand out include a two-for-four outing against the Browns on May 14; a three-for-six-with-a-pair-of-doubles afternoon in a 9-0 romp of Cleveland on May 22; and a three-for-four-with-a-triple-and-two-runs-scored performance in a come-from-behind 3-2 win over the Brownies on June 10. And, looking back from today's perspective, Larry would have greatly admired a string of victories over the Yankees – disliked intensely now; merely a lowly league member then – toward the end of June. The Sox trimmed the Hilltoppers (the Yankees' then other nickname/they played at Hilltop Park), 5-2, in New York on June 19. It was their fifth straight win over the New Yorkers that season. Admitted *The Times*: "Beating the Yankees has become a habit with

the Boston Red Sox." And the Sox did it again – twice – on June 22. The first contest saw Larry go three for four with a triple as the Bostonians trimmed the New Yorkers, 13-2. Game two of the twinbill had Larry go one for three with two runs scored in a 10-8 Sox triumph. The Yanks still had not won a single 1912 game against Larry, Tris Speaker, Harry Hooper, Duffy Lewis, Bill Carrigan and company. (Ed. note: it would not be until July 2 that the Hilltoppers finally took one, 9-7, from the Red Sox; and that in spite of Larry going three for four).

Other games of note that wonderful Red Sox season of 1912 included a victory over the White Sox on July 19, an 8-0 game that saw Larry get three hits in four trips to the plate in support of former fellow University of Vermont teammate Ray Collins; a two-for-four performance by Larry in a 6-3 win over the Cleveland Naps (better known now as the "Indians"), with Smoky Joe Wood (spelled "Wod" in the day's wire service write-up) getting the decision; a four for five outing in another win, 8-6, over the Naps; a 4-3 game over the Tigers on August 19, of which it was written in *The Times* that "Gardner fielded spectacularly at third base;" and yet another doubleheader win over the moribund Yankees, 2-1 and 1-0, on September 2. In a year of streaks, Joe Wood won his 14th straight – and 30th overall – in the second game, while Hugh Bedient – on the way to his only 20-game season with the Red Sox or anyone else – took the opener. Larry was four for seven for the day.

THIRD BASE

When the infield dust finally settled, it was the Red Sox and the New York Giants in the Fall Classic. And a classic it was to be, indeed. *The New York Times*, as a circulation booster, hired a noted sportswriter-of-the-day named Hugh S. Fullerton to rate both teams, position-by-position/player-by-player. At third he gave a very definite nod to Larry over the Giants' Buck Herzog. Fullerton was not subtle: he wrote "Gardner looms up as so much better a player as to make Herzog appear as a minor leaguer." The writer similarly ranked most of the other positions in Boston's favor, adding that "New York's best chance to win this series is to wait out Boston's pitchers and get hit by pitched balls." *The Times* billed Mr. Fullerton as "one of the foremost baseball critics in the country." Giant fans billed him less kindly. A person who signed his letter to the paper "A Polo Grounder" called Fullerton's writing "junk." "A Loyal Fan" called it "bum dope." A Giant rooter named O'Toole suggested Mr. Fullerton was a "sorehead," while another Giants' supporter suggested that Hugh would be far better off following a career as a dishwasher than as a writer. And a Mr. William P. DeGraw perhaps best summed up New York fan sentiment when he closed his letter regarding Mr. Fullerton with a "Pish! Tush! and a couple of pooh-poohs!"

Mr. Fullerton's views aside, John McGraw and his Giants did not roll over and play dead. The first game went to Boston by the narrow margin of 4-3, with the Sox "using their hits with the thrift of a Vermont housewife," as Frederick G. Lieb so colorfully phrased it in his THE BOSTON RED SOX. Smoky Joe struck out eleven and was tough when he had to be. Game two ended up a 6-6 tie after eleven innings when darkness came to Fenway. (Ed. note: the game was never completed. The score is still 6-6.). Rube Marquard brought the Giants back in game three, outpitching Brockton-native Buck O'Brien, 2-1. A splendid running catch by Giant rightfielder Josh Devore of a long fly ball off the bat of catcher Hick Cady with two on and two out in the bottom of the ninth saved the day for the New Yorkers. Game four saw Larry come to life. The thirdsacker drilled a single and a triple, walked once, and scored twice as Smoky Joe again bested the McGrawmen, 3-1. The game was played before 36,502 at the Polo Grounds, with at least 2,500 additional fans watching for free from the vantage point of Coogan's Bluff rising above the stadium, and a third crowd gathered in Times Square to follow the game via *The Times*' electric scoreboard.

Game five saw another 2-1 tight one. Only this time the Bostons won, with ace rookie Hugh Bedient tossing a three-hitter to beat the one-and-only Christy Mathewson. Their backs to the wall, the Giants took games six and seven by scores of 5-2 and 11-4. In Game six the New Yorkers scored a quick five runs off Buck O'Brien in the first inning. In game seven they jumped all over Smoky Joe Wood and Charley Hall, amassing 16 hits including three doubles and a two-run homer by Giant secondbaseman Larry Doyle. It was a big day for "Larrys:" Larry Gardner also hit a circuit clout (the only one for the Bosox in the entire Series).

So the stage was set. One game for all the glory. It was a game that turned out to be monumental. New York jumped out to a 1-0 lead in the third when Giant leftfielder Red Murray hit a shot that barely eluded a hobbling Tris Speaker, scoring Josh Devore from third. The Red Sox came back with one in the seventh. Innings eight and nine saw no change as Peerless Matty and Smoky Joe set 'em down. In the top of the tenth a double by Murray and a single by firstbaseman Fred Merkle put the Giants in the lead. Three outs and the Series was New York's. For the Sox it was Smoky Joe leading off. The fine-hitting Wood, however, had injured his hand knocking down a line drive in the Giants' tenth. Manager Jake Stahl sent reserve infielder Clyde Engle into the game to pinch hit. Engle, no slugger, lofted an easy fly to Giants' centerfielder Fred Snodgrass...who caught it and then "uncaught" it. He let the ball slip through the fingers of his glove. "Write in the pages of World Series baseball history the name of Snodgrass. Write it large and black," dramatically wrote *The Times* on their front page the next day. Engle wound up on second, the result of the error that has forever tainted Fred Snodgrass. The outfielder, however, is tainted at least somewhat unjustly. The very next batter for the Sox, Harry Hooper, drove a long liner to center that Mr. Snodgrass hauled in on the dead run. A marvelous catch. Matty then walked secondbase-

man Steve Yerkes, bringing up the perennially-dangerous Tris Speaker. The Gray Eagle proceeded to hit a humble pop-up in first base foul territory. Either Matty or Fred Merkle could have caught it. Barehanded. But neither did. Tris repaid the favor by smashing a long single to right, scoring Engle and sending Yerkes to third. John McGraw elected to intentionally walk Duffy Lewis to set up a double play possibility. It was a mistake. Next up was – as you might guess – Larry Gardner. And the man from Vermont promptly propelled a long fly to right field, deep enough to score Yerkes from third and deep enough to again make Boston the capital of the baseball world.

What's left after being a World Champ? In Larry Gardner's case, the answer was "plenty." While the Bosox were denied pennants in 1913 (with Larry slipping to .281 and the Sox slipping to fourth) and 1914 (.259 and second), they came charging back to capture first in 1915 and 1916. Larry hit his Red Sox low of .258 in 1915 but upped that a resounding fifty points, to .308, in 1916. Led by the batting of Tris Speaker (.322) and Duffy Lewis (.291) and the pitching of Rube Foster (19-8), Ernie Shore (also 19-8), Dutch Leonard (15-7), Joe Wood (15-5), and a newcomer by the name of George Herman "Babe" Ruth (18-8), the Bosox edged out Ty Cobb, Bobby Veach, and Sam Crawford and the Detroit Tigers for the 1915 AL flag. Led by the batting of Larry Gardner (with Tris Speaker traded to the Indians at the start of the season, Larry found himself, at .308, the only player on the Red Sox

THIRD BASE

Circa 1916 photo

Larry, left, and Babe Ruth, when both were with the Red Sox. Larry was the man holding down third when Ruth made his big-league debut on July 11, 1914, pitching six strong innings in a 4-3 win over Cleveland. Larry had three of the Sox' eight hits that day, including a triple. It was a nice way to welcome the big guy to Boston.

But the thirdbaseman wasn't always so obliging. Early-on he discovered that the Babe, per Robert W. Smith in his 1983 book, BASEBALL IN THE AFTERNOON, was afraid of snakes or "anything that wiggled." And, again per Robert W. Smith, Larry "could send the big man screaming across the outfield by threatening him with a caterpillar."

Circa 1916 photo

55

team to hit over .275 in 1916) and the pitching of the Babe (23-12), Dutch Leonard (18-12), Carl Mays (18-13), Ernie Shore (16-10), and Rube Foster (14-7), the Bosox edged out Eddie Collins, Happy Felsch, and Joe Jackson and the Chicago White Sox for the 1916 AL flag. In both seasons the managing of Lewiston, Maine's Bill Carrigan (see pages 128-133) had much to do with the Red Sox success. On that score there was *no* disagreement.

As in 1912, Larry contributed his share as the Red Sox easily defeated the Philadelphia Phillies in 1915. Managed most ably by Fitchburg native son Pat Moran, the Phils had slugger Gavvy Cravath (whose 24 home runs and 115 RBIs were both the best in the National League by a wide margin) and the bedazzling Grover Cleveland Alexander (whose 31 wins and 1.22 ERA also both led the National League by a wide margin) and not too much else. The Phils took the first game, with Gavvy driving in the winning run and Grover scattering eight hits. That was it for the Moranmen. Game two went to the Red Sox, 2-1, with Larry, who was two for four, scoring the winning run in the ninth. "He galloped home with the victory," descriptively wrote Bill Carrigan's local paper, the *Lewiston Evening Journal.* Games three, four, and five were all decided by one run. But that one run always belonged to Boston. In the final contest Harry Hooper hit two home runs, Duffy Lewis, one, and Larry added a triple as the Sox turned on the power. Final score in games: Boston, five, and

Circa 1920 photograph

After playing in three World Series with the Red Sox, the Pride of Enosburg Falls got to play in a fourth when he batted .310 and drove in 118 runs to lead the Indians to their first-ever American League flag in 1920.

THIRD BASE

Philadelphia, one. The Red Sox were World Champs once more.

In 1916 the Red Sox squared off with the Dodgers for the Championship of the World. As with the Phils in 1915, the Sox were just too good for their National League opponent. Often called the "Robins" (in honor of their colorful manager, Wilbert "Uncle Robbie" Robinson), Brooklyn was anchored by Jake Daubert (.316) and Zack Wheat (.312) offensively, and Jeff Pfeffer (25-11) on the mound. A young Charles Dillon "Casey" Stengel (.279) was on hand too, but as an outfielder rather than a manager. The Sox began by taking the first two games, 6-5 and 2-1. More than 40,000 fans turned out for both contests, played in Boston at Braves Field rather than Fenway Park (see page 107). The pride of Colby College, Jack Coombs, saved the Robins from total dishonor by stopping the Sox, 4-3, in game three, played at Ebbets Field. Colby Jack didn't have the sweeping curve he'd had with the Athletics in 1910-1912, but he still had enough stuff to fool most of the Red Sox most of the time. One he didn't fool, however, was Larry. In the seventh the thirdsacker drove a Coombs' pitch over the right field wall and out of the park onto Bedford Avenue (later, in the 1950s, to be the happy landing ground for many of Duke Snider's shots).

In game four Mr. Gardner again turned on the power. The Robins had tallied twice in the first, but Larry more than countered that by slamming a three-run center field homer in the Sox second off future Hall-of-Famer Rube Marquard. "The blow was the hardest and longest struck in the series," wrote *The Times*, adding that it "turned the joy of Brooklyn's supporters into despair." Even old friend Hugh S. Fullerton was impressed. He called the shot "the most terrific drive of the series." The homer also seemed to take whatever starch the Brooklyn ballclub yet had and cause it to vanish. The Robins scored no more in the fourth game and scored but once in the Series' finale, game five. Bill Carrigan and his Boston boys of summer had won back-to-back World Championships. Headlined *The New York Times*: "Robins completely Outclassed and American League Team Has an Easy Time." Headlined the *Lewiston Evening Journal*: "Bill Carrigan For Mayor Says Latest Report."

Vermont's all-time all-star infielder played one more season for the Red Sox, batting a respectable .265 in 1917. Then it was bye bye, Boston/hello, Philadelphia. Larry, along with outfielder Clarence "Tilly" Walker and reserve catcher Hick Cady, was traded to the Athletics for Stuffy McInnis. Larry was not to get to know the City of Brotherly Love too awfully well, though: after but one season – in which he played in 127 games and upped his average to .285 – Larry was off to Cleveland. For the Tribe he strung together three bang-up years in a row. He hit .300 in 1919; .310 in 1920; .319 in 1921. But it was not just Larry's batting average that pleased: he knocked in 118 runs in 1920 and 115 in 1921, while also scoring 101 runs in 1921. His 118 RBIs in 1920 was good for fifth in the league. Only Babe Ruth (137),

Baby Doll Jacobson (122), George Sisler (also 122), and Joe Jackson (121) had more runners knocked in than the Cleveland thirdbaseman. Larry's old Boston teammate – and now Cleveland teammate and manager – Tris Speaker, had 107 RBIs.

With Cleveland, Larry got to play in his fourth and final World Series. How many players get to play in four World Series? The answer, apart from too many Yankees, is not many. It was Cleveland's first World Series; the Dodgers' second. With a line-up that featured six .300 hitters, including Tris Speaker at .388, the Indians were favored. The Dodgers, led by outfielder Zack Wheat (.328) and veteran spitballer Burleigh Grimes (23-11), surprised by taking two of the first three games. Then Tris Speaker's mother came to town. Mrs. Speaker made the trip all the way from her home in Hubbard City, Texas. She told the press that Tris was a "good boy" and always obeyed her while he was growing up in Texas, and that she expected him to now do likewise regarding the matter at hand. And that matter at hand was to beat Brooklyn.

Was it Mrs. Speaker's presence? Or was it fate? Whatever, the Tribe took the next four straight to win the best-of-nine series, five games to two. One of those four-straight games is yet recalled. It was game five, played in Cleveland on October 10. To start with, Indians' rightfielder Elmer Smith hit the first grand slam homer in World Series history. He did it right off, too, blasting a Grimes' first-inning pitch over the right field fence; thereby becoming, in the words of *The New York Times*, a personage right up there "alongside the famous Smiths of history, which include Captain John, the Smith Brothers (of cough drop fame), and the Village Smithy." Then the Indians' star moundsman, Jim Bagby (31-12 during the season), sent a two-run shot into the stands in the fourth; the first pitcher to ever hit a homer in a Series' game. Overshadowing both feats, however, was a play pulled off by Cleveland secondbaseman Bill Wambsganss in the fifth inning. The Robins had runners on first and second. Uncle Robbie called for a hit and run. Batter Clarence Mitchell obliged. He stung a line shot seemingly headed over second into center field. Suddenly, however, Wamby was on the scene. "With a mighty jump (he) speared the ball with one hand," wrote *The Times*. Upon returning to earth the agile secondbaseman noticed that the runner who'd been on second, Pete Kilduff, was still moving toward third. Wamby put an end to that by stepping on second. He then further noticed ("Wamby's noodle began to operate faster than it ever did before:" *The Times*) that the runner who'd been on first, Otto Miller, was frozen in his tracks just short of second. (He was "standing there like a wooden Indian:" again *The Times*). Wamby strolled over and tagged him. Voila: an unassisted triple play. There has never been another in Series' history.

Following his trio of bang-up seasons, 1919-1921, Larry slipped somewhat, to .285, in 1922. By baseball standards he was getting old. In

1923, aged 37, Larry's playing time slipped to 52 games and but 79 at-bats. His average decreased as well, to .253. Those weren't bad numbers, though, compared to 1924. In that him. In 1929 the old pro accepted a position as physical education teacher and coach at his alma mater, the University of Vermont. There he would remain for 23 years, until 1952, also

---

QUIZ TIME

Let's close with a short quiz. One that's not too difficult.

Who holds the all-time record for homers by a Red Sox thirdbaseman in World Series play?

Who, in fact, is the ONLY Red Sox thirdbaseman to have ever hit a homer in World Series play?

For answers please turn upside down:

....

That's right: only one thirdbaseman in Red Sox history has hit a home run in a World Series. And that thirdbaseman – William Lawrence Gardner – has hit three of 'em.

---

year the veteran played just eight games at third and six at second. He also pinch hit 22 times. The totals: ten hits in 50 at-bats, which worked out to a rather unglamorous .200. Larry decided his professional playing career was over. His involvement with baseball, though, was not. Far from it. Larry's first stop was managing Dallas in the Texas League. Then it was on to Asheville, North Carolina in the Piedmont League. But Vermont called to

serving as the school's athletic director the last six years. Larry, as well, was active in campaigning for players' rights, especially those of retired players. He was commissioner of the old Northern League for a number of years. And he did some fishing, too.

Larry Gardner, "the Diving Thirdbaseman," died at the home of his son, William Lawrence Gardner, Jr., in St. George, Vermont on March 11, 1976.

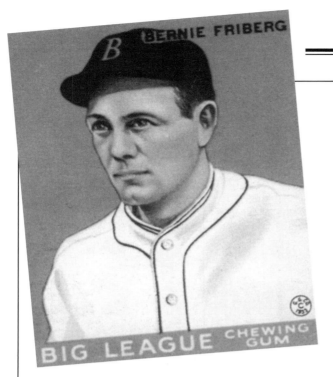

I'm going to cheat somewhat and include
AUGUSTAF BERNHARDT "BERNIE" FRIBERG,
portrayed here on a 1933 Big League Chewing Gum card, in the book because he's a New England ballplayer who should be remembered. Born in Manchester, New Hampshire on August 18, 1899, he died in Swampscott, Massachusetts on December 8, 1958. Played 14 years in the bigs, 1919-1920 and 1922-1933, mostly with the Cubs and the Phillies. Was at home at all four infield positions and the outfield, and could wallop the ball, too. Best season was 1930 when clicked for a .341 average, but also batted over .300 in 1922, 1923, 1929, and 1933. The latter season was, alas, his only time in a Boston uniform. But he made it count, hitting .317 in 17 games for the Red Sox. Lifetime is .281 in 1299 games.

HARRY DONALD LORD,
portrayed here on a 1910 Sweet Caporal Cigarettes card, was born in Porter, Maine on March 8, 1882 and died in Westbrook, Maine on August 9, 1948. Was a baseball star at both Bridgton (Maine) Academy and Bates College. Planned to be a lawyer but realized was more money in baseball. Played for Worcester in New England League and Providence in International League before advancing to Red Sox in 1907. Held down hot corner for Boston, 1908-1910; then White Sox, 1910-1914. Was player-manager of Buffalo in the Federal League in 1915. Best seasons were 1909 when hit .311 with 36 stolen bases and 85 runs scored for Bosox, and 1911 when hit .321 with 43 stolen bases and 103 runs scored for Chisox. Lifetime is .278 in 972 games.

LORD BOSTON & CH'GO AMER.

JOSEPH ALBERT ARMAND "SKIPPY" ROBERGE,

shown here in a circa 1946 photo, was born in Lowell, Massachusetts on May 19, 1917 and died in Lowell on June 7, 1993. Was a star in football and basketball as well as baseball at Lowell's Keith Academy. Played for Bradford, Pennsylvania, Evansville, Indiana, and Hartford, Connecticut in minors before joining Braves in 1941. First manager with Braves was Casey Stengel.

Always the comedian, Stengel once filled Skippy's glove with pebbles as a practical joke. Was in the army, 1943-1945. Wounded in Germany in 1945, came back to have his most successful season, 1946, batting .231 in 48 games for the Braves. Lifetime is .220 in 177 games.

EDWARD CHARLES "EDDIE" PELLAGRINI,

shown here in a circa 1947 photo, was born in Boston on March 13, 1918 and died in Boston, October 11, 1989. Played eight seasons in the majors, two each with Red Sox, Pirates, and Browns, and one each with Phillies and Reds, 1946-1954. Greatest distinction may have been a home run in his first major league at-bat, for the Red Sox against the Senators, April 22, 1946. Would, though, go on to hit but 19 more during his major league career. More of a shortstop than a thirdsacker, but did play mostly third for Sox and that's where we have him here. Best season was 1953 when batted .253 in 78 games with the Pirates. Lifetime is .226 in 563 games.

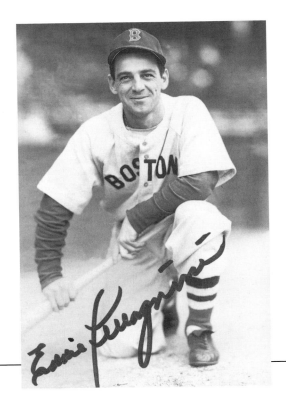

William Joseph "Bill" Barrett

There have been close to a dozen "big league Barretts" – players with the surname "Barrett" – in the majors. What's surprising is that virtually all of them have had a New England connection. First to come to mind is Marty Barrett, who played a stellar second for the Sox in the 1980s. Then there's Johnny Barrett, a Lowell native who played outfield for the Pirates and Braves in the 1940s; Jimmy Barrett, an Athol native who was a flyhawk for the Sox and three other teams at the dawn of the 20th century; Bob Barrett, a teammate of Bill's on the 1929 Bosox; Charlie "Red" Barrett, a pitcher who won eleven games for the 1947 Braves; even Tommy Barrett, Marty's brother, who had "a cup of coffee" with the Phils and the Red Sox; others. Most of all, though, there's William Joseph "Bill" Barrett, who played a lot of outfield, some infield, and even did a little pitching, too, in nine seasons with the Athletics, White Sox, Red Sox, and Senators.

Born in Cambridge, Massachusetts on May 28, 1900, Bill was a schoolboy star at Cambridge's Rindge Technical. While he excelled at all positions, it was his pitching that at first attracted attention and led to Bill's being signed by Connie Mack's Philadelphia

Athletics upon his graduation from Rindge in June of 1917. After a number of seasons in the minors, Bill found himself in Philadelphia in 1921. With the Mackmen that summer, Bill appeared in fourteen games spread over four positions: shortstop, third base, first base, and, of course, pitcher. Not knowing where best to play Bill, Connie took a time-honored route: he shipped the Pride of Cambridge back to the minors, to Moline in the Illinois-Iowa-Indiana (Three-I) League, and then to Reading in the International League. It would not be until 1923 that Bill would make his way back to the Show; this time as a position player, and this time with the White Sox, the team with which he would remain for most of his playing career.

For the Pale Hose, Bill batted .272 in 42 games in 1923. He upped that to 119 games in 1924, knocking out a .271 average while playing short, third, and the outfield. In 1925 the versatile performer appeared in far fewer games, 81, but hit a resounding .363, while playing both the infield and the outfield. In 1926 Bill played in 111 games and finally settled into the outfield for good. He again hit over .300, getting 113 hits in 368 at-bats for a .307 mark.

That brings us to 1927. For most baseball fans, 1927 was the year of the Yankees. In fact, the '27 Yankees are considered by many to be the best baseball team of all time. And for good reason: the Yankee line-up that year featured Lou Gehrig (.373/47/175), Earle Combs

OUTFIELD

(.356/6/64), Bob Meusel (.337/8/103), Tony Lazzeri (.309/18/102), and pitchers Waite Hoyt (22-7), Wilcy Moore (19-7), Herb Pennock (19-8), Urban Shocker (18-6), and George Pipgras (10-3). And, oh yes, Babe Ruth. All the Sultan of Swat did that memorable season was bat .356, drive in 164 runs, and blast his earthshattering 60 home runs. The Bronx Bombers ran away with the American League pennant and then trounced the Pirates four straight in the World Series.

But 1927 was also, in many ways, Bill

Circa 1927 photo

A jack of all trades, Bill Barrett played every outfield and infield position, plus doing a little pitching as well, during his nine-year stay in the majors.

Barrett's most satisfying year. Cambridge Bill played in all but seven of the White Sox's 153 games, batted a strong .286, and drove in a hefty 83 runs even though he hit but four homers. So it seemed like it might be interesting to see how the Chisox, who finished fifth with a won-lost record of 70-83, fared versus the mighty Yankees (who finished at 110-44).

crowd of 55,000 at Comiskey, was much the same. The only difference: the score was 9-0, Yankees. Gehrig had no more home runs, but he did weigh in with a pair of triples. Bill again collected a double and a single. The White Sox managed to take the third game of the series, 2-1, in ten innings. Veteran Sox hurler Urban Faber did a fine job of quieting the Yank's big

Bill Barrett was one of the game's great bench jockeys...so adroit at this secondary calling that a Chicago sportswriter of the day advised White Sox fans – not completely tongue-in-cheek – to wear earmuffs to Comiskey Park when the Yankees came to town. That was because "Whispering Bill" especially loved to voice his views to the Yanks' home run duo, the Babe and Lou Gehrig. And he had a voice that resounded. And resounded. And resounded.

The White Sox started out well that season of seasons. They were "going fast," as a *New York Times'* writer put it. In fact, the White Sox were in second, just behind the New Yorkers, when they first played the Yankees.

In the teams' first encounter, in Chicago before 35,000 chilled fans on May 7, Yankee mainstay Herb Pennock shut out the White Sox, 8-0, while Lou Gehrig walloped a grand slam into Comiskey Park's new right field pavilion. Bill Barrett, batting third for Chicago, hit a double and a single in three trips to the plate. Game two, watched by an overflow

bats (Ruth was 0 for 3, while Larruping Lou was held to one triple), as Bill (who was three for four) and his mates posted the win.

At the onset of the two teams' second series, in New York in early June, Chicago was still in second, close on the heels of the Yankees. Not for long. Ruth and Gehrig both slammed homers in game one. As The *Times'* James R. Harrison wrote: "Alphonse Thomas (a rookie White Sox pitcher who went into the game with a mark of 10-2) learned that G. Herman Ruth and H. Louis Gehrig do not lug their bats to the plate merely in order to con-

OUTFIELD

May 1929 cartoon

It was just like coming home when Bill was traded to the Red Sox in May of 1929. He rewarded his new team with a solid .270 in 111 games.

form to the rules." The final score was 4-1, New York, with Bill going one for four. Game two was a slugfest, with the New Yorkers tallying five times in the ninth inning and then taking the game in the eleventh. Tony Lazzeri homered three times for the Yanks while Bill, moved to the clean-up slot, came through with a homer himself. Game number three saw the Bombers score six in the seventh, the Babe pull a steal of home, and an 8-3 New York victory. Bill went 0 for 4. As in the first series between the two, the Sox managed to stave off total defeat by taking the series' finale, 4-2, for Ted Lyons' eighth straight win. Bill had a double, a single, and a run scored.

By the time the two clubs went at it again,

in late July, the White Sox were in the slot they would hold for the rest of the year, fifth, while the Hugmen were just continuing to roll along. Highlights from the remainder of the season – for either team – included a four-for-four effort by Bill in a 7-5 Chicago victory on July 22; Ruth's 31st fourbagger plus a triple as the Yankees topped the Sox, 3-2, on July 24; another Ted Lyons' win, 6-3, on August 6; and the contest of August 16, in which the Bambino hit the first ball ever to sail clear out of Comiskey Park. Penned *The Times*' Chicago correspondent: "In the fifth inning, Babe crashed into one of Alphonse Thomas' fast balls and made it faster."

There was more. Lots more. But the end

result was generally predictable: Ruth and Gehrig homers and New York victories. For every Chicago run, the Bronx Bombers, or so it seemed, would score two. Or three. The final count was eighteen wins for New York and four wins for Chicago. And Bill? The man from the north side of the Charles ended at .309 (25 for 81) against the Yanks. The Pirates could have used him in the Series.

The year of 1928 was a downer for Bill. He played in but 76 games as the White Sox altered their line-up in an attempt to break out of fifth place, the position they'd held since 1924 (Ed. note: they did not succeed). On the bright side, however, less playing time for Bill undoubtedly gave him more of an opportunity to live up to his sometimes nickname of "Whispering Bill." Bill, you see, was a bench jockey almost without peer. He reputedly had a voice so voluminous that, as one Chicago sportswriter of the day, Hal Totten, quipped: "Bill's lowest whisper rattles the windows of the Wentworth avenue (trolley) cars as they pass a block east of the park. If you don't believe it," continued Mr. Totten at least somewhat tongue-in-cheek, "ride in one and listen to the rattle. In fact, natives claim that the echoes keep the windows rattling all the rest of the day." Jesting one step further, the Chicago scribe advised the wearing of earmuffs by fans when the Yankees came to town…for that's when Mr. Bill was at his peak of vocal power and, oh, how he loved to harass Mssrs. Ruth and Gehrig.

The tumultuous year of 1929 – the year of the crash – saw many notable baseball headlines. A sampling could well include: "Ruth Hits 500th Home Run," or "Miller Huggins Dies," or "Giants Install Baseball's First Public Address System in Polo Grounds," or "Barrett Traded to Red Sox; Cambridge Player Comes Home."

No, the latter probably wouldn't really rank high on a newsworthy scale. But it ranks high here. The Pride of Rindge Tech was traded to the Red Sox on May 23. It was an even swap of outfielders: Bill in exchange for Doug Taitt, then in his second year with the Bosox.

Was Whispering Bill delighted? You may be certain of it. The trade did produce box score problems, though: the Sox already had a B. Barrett on the team in the person of thirdbaseman Bob Barrett. Then there was outfielder Russ Scarritt. Fans couldn't just glance at a Sox box score anymore. They had to concentrate.

Bill settled right in with the Bosox. Sometimes he played left field, sometimes right. It would be wonderful to say that, with him in the line-up, the Sox charged up the standings and threatened the all-powerful Athletics and Yankees. But, no, the Sox didn't even really much challenge the seventh-place White Sox. Cambridge Bill, though, had some fun and some fine games. He scored a run in a 5-4 Red Sox win over the Athletics on May 28. It was especially memorable because it halted an Athletics' eleven-game winning streak. And because the A's had been ahead, 4-0. Two days later, on May 30, Bill went three for four against the same Athletics. Off Lefty Grove, no less. This time, however, the Mackmen reigned supreme, 9-2. With a line-up that included Jimmie Foxx, Al Simmons, Bing Miller, Mule Haas, and Bridgewater, Massachusetts' own Mickey Cochrane, they usually did.

A big surprise to many in 1929 was the fall of the Yankees, winners of the Junior Circuit flag the previous three seasons. Star hurlers Herb Pennock and Waite Hoyt never really got on track. And the Babe came down with a celebrated cold in very early June; disappeared, per *The New York Times*, in "a big black limousine" for a respite with Mrs. Ruth on June 11; did not get back into the starting line-up until June 20. Upon his return, Babe told the press that, while the Athletics had been "playing great ball," they "are bound to crack sooner or later." Such was a sentiment not shared by Connie Mack. On June 28, his team up ten games on the Yanks, Connie told attendees at a Germantown (Pennsylvania) Business Men's Association luncheon that "Only accidents or an earthquake will stop us." (Ed. note: at that very same luncheon Connie also stated that he had no immediate plans to retire from the game he loved. "I intend to stick," as he worded it, "to that little game of baseball." And indeed he did. It would, in fact, be another 21 seasons before "The Tall Tactician" stepped down as Athletics' manager.).

Other 1929 games which Whispering Bill enjoyed in what, for all intents and purposes was his last in the majors, included a contest against the Yankees on July 3 in which he went two for four with a double and a run scored. Then there was the game of July 11, won by the Sox, 15-8, over Detroit in Detroit. Bill contributed a double and a run scored in three at-bats in what would have been an even bigger rout had not the Tigers executed a triple play in the seventh. Another favorite with Bill was undoubtedly a game against his former team, the White Sox, on August 2. Bill knocked in the tying run in the tenth with a double; then scored the winning tally in a 3-2 squeaker as teammate Bill Regan singled him home.

Whistling Bill did all right by both the Red Sox and himself in 1929. In 111 games for the Sox, he'd hit a solid .270, all the while playing a strong and steady outfield. It, alas, was to be his swan song. After a slow start (.167 average in six games), Bill was traded to the Washington Senators for lifetime .306 hitter Earl Webb (see page 92). For the Nats, Bill did even worse (an .000 average in six games). The result: Bill was released to Minneapolis in the American Association. He never made it back to the bigs. But he didn't quit easily. After Minneapolis, Bill played for Kansas City (then also in the American Association), Reading, New Haven, and Shreveport before packing up his suitcase and coming home in 1935.

Back in Cambridge, Bill became a sales promotion manager for Seagram Distillers, and a longtime member of the city's recreation commission. He was also a Red Sox scout.

Bill Barrett collapsed and died of a heart attack at his home at 35 Huron Avenue on January 26, 1951. Among those who attended his funeral were such legends as Eddie Collins, Joe Cronin, Hugh Duffy, and Johnny Pesky.

John Francis "Shano" Collins

John Francis "Shano" Collins was a true son of Massachusetts. He was born and raised in the shadow of Boston, in Charlestown. Yet he later called Pittsfield, which is definitely not in the shadow of Boston, home as well. Shano also had a split allegiance with respect to team loyalty. He spent the first eleven seasons of his lengthy playing career with the White Sox (including 1919 when he was a part of the "Clean Sox"), and the latter four with the Red Sox. Sort of a reverse Carlton Fisk. He also had somewhat of a split allegiance with respect to his position. Most years he was an outfielder. But in 1911 and especially 1920, he was a firstbaseman. Toss in two years as Red Sox manager, in 1931-1932, and you behold a man with quite the substantial major league medley indeed.

John Collins was born in Charlestown on December 4, 1885. A standout semi-pro performer in his late teens, he entered organized ball with Haverhill in the New England League in 1907, playing 15 games at shortstop and batting .266. From there he moved to Springfield in the Connecticut League, playing second and hitting an impressive .322 in 88 games. At the close of the 1909 season, Shano (a derivation of "Sean," Gaelic for "John") was pur-

chased by the White Sox. With the Pale Hose, the Massachusetts' native was primarily an outfielder. And a sure and steady one with glue in his glove, a far-reaching range, and a strong and accurate throwing arm. His bat was sure and steady, too. Although no Ty Cobb or George Sisler, Shano could be counted upon to hit in the range of .270, higher in the clutch. He knocked in 81 runs while batting .292 for the 1912 White Sox. In 1915, although he had a puny .257 average, he knocked in 85 runners. That same year also saw Shano, a bit of a speedster, steal a career-high 38 bases.

In 1917, the White Sox won their first AL flag since the Tinker-to-Evers-to-Chance Sox of 1906. It would be nice to proclaim that Shano was the key ingredient in his team's success. But it wouldn't be true. Shano was platooned with another veteran outfielder, Nemo Leibold, in right field. Left-handed hitting Nemo saw action against right-handed pitchers, while right-handed-hitting Shano made the line-up against the less-prevalent lefties. They were quite a "couple." Nemo, who stood 5'6", was often referred to as "little." Shano, who stood an even 6', was never referred to as "little." And, while platooning may have been good for the team, it didn't do much for either outfielder. Leibold hit a weak .236; Shano an even weaker .234.

Even a .234 hitter, however, has some big games. For Shano, in 1917, these would

OUTFIELD

Circa 1917 photo

A swift and sure outfielder and a steady performer at the plate, John "Shano" Collins was a "Sox Man:" he played eleven seasons for the White Sox, four for the Red Sox. He managed the Bosox in 1931-1932 as well.

include an 8-3 win over the Indians on May 2 which saw Shano go four for five, including a triple and two runs scored; another game against the Tribe, June 24, in which Shano drove in the afternoon's only run in a 1-0 duel; a 4-3 win over the Tigers on July 4, with Shano rapping out a single, double, and triple and scoring half his team's runs (and Ty Cobb singling, to extend his consecutive-game hitting streak to 34); a perfect four-for-four and four runs scored as the Chisox took the Yankees, 8-3, on August 26; and, perhaps most meaningful of all, the game of September 21 in which Shano drove in catcher Ray Schalk with the winning run in a 2-1 ten-inning thriller vs. the Red Sox…and that gave the White Sox their long-awaited third American League pennant.

The Series of 1917 promised to be a fan's delight. The National League's pacesetters, John McGraw's New York Giants, were led by former Federal League star Benny Kauff (.308) and leftfielder George Burns (.302) offensively, and by Ferdinand "Ferdie" Schupp (21-7), Harry "Slim" Sallee (18-7), Pol Perritt (17-7), and Rube Benton (15-9) on the mound. For the Chisox it was outfielders Happy Felsch (.308), Joe Jackson (.301), and secondbaseman Eddie Collins (.289) at the plate, and Eddie Cicotte (28-12), Urban "Red" Faber (16-13), and Claude "Lefty" Williams (17-8) doing the bulk of the pitching.

With southpaw Slim Sallee on the hill for the McGrawmen in game number one, Chicago manager Clarence "Pants" Rowland started Shano in right. It was a good move: the Charlestown native went a tidy three for four while scoring one of Chicago's two tallies in a 2-1 White Sox win. Shano also started game two, but was only in the line-up long enough to go 0 for 1 – he hit an infield pop-up – before being replaced by Nemo Leibold. The Sox went on to take the game, Shano or no Shano, as they scored five runs in the fourth on their way to a 7-2 Red Faber victory. Game three saw the Giants finally break into the win column as John "Rube" Benton shut out the Sox – and Shano, who was 0 for 4. The Sox were stifled again in game four, losing 5-0 to Ferdie Schupp. Benny Kauff hit two homers for New York. Shano was two for four. Game five, played in Chicago, saw the White Sox fall behind, 4-1; then come back to score three in the seventh and three in the eighth to win, 8-5. Shano scored what was the winning run in the eighth. He opened the inning with a single, moved to second on a sacrifice by thirdbaseman Fred McMullin, scored on a single to center by Eddie Collins. Wrote *The New York Times*: "The rooters went wild with delight, and the White Sox players performed a dance in front of the dugout." Game six saw the end of the Series of 1917. Shano went 0 for 3, but the Sox capitalized on three Giant errors to take the championship by a score of 4-2. After the game Giant manager McGraw told White Sox manager Rowland that the Sox had beaten the Giants with "as game and fair a team as he had ever played against."

Sandwiched between the pennant-winning season of 1917 and the to-come pennant-winning season of 1919 there came 1918. It was not a year that would be cherished by White Sox fans. Not only did the Sox fall out of first place; they fell completely out of the first division. To sixth. World War I was in high gear. In his 1919 book, COMMY: THE LIFE STORY OF CHARLES A. COMISKEY, author G. W. Axelson summed up the season of 1918 by penning: "Shot to pieces by enlistments and drafts the White Sox failed to make any kind of showing during the season of 1918." Joe Jackson took a job with the Harlan and Hollingsworth Shipbuilding Company, located in Wilmington, Delaware. He played in but seventeen games for the 1918 Sox. Future Hall of Fame pitcher Red Faber found himself doing his throwing for the Great Lakes Naval Training Station. He played in zero games for the 1918 Sox. Other team members missed part of the season as well. Shano appeared in 103 of that summer's war-shortened 124-game schedule, batting .274.

With the war over and Joe Jackson back to reclaim his outfield berth in 1919, Shano once more found himself platooning with Nemo Leibold in right field. The result: he took part in only 63 games. Unlike 1917, when platooning had dulled his batting eye, though, the man from Massachusetts hit a relatively robust .279 that fateful season. And, come World Series time, he was stationed in right for the opener against Edd Roush, Heinie Groh, and the rest of the Cincinnati Reds.

Entire books have been written about the World Series of 1919 – the "Black Sox" Series.

Shano played in half of the Series' eight games (it was a five-out-of-nine set-to), going four for 16, which works to a humble .250. He did, though, endear himself to Chisox rooters with his game seven performance. He went three for five with a double and two runs scored in a 4-1 Pale Hose victory. It was the second and last Chicago win. Starting Sox hurler Lefty Williams was hammered the next day and the Reds were World Champions. Stated Reds' manager – and Fitchburg native – Pat Moran: "The Reds are champions and I am the happiest man in the world tonight. I cannot praise my players too highly. They played remarkable ball, fought every minute to win, and there never was a time when they lost confidence." Stated White Sox manager Kid Gleason: "They (the Reds) beat us in one of the greatest series ever staged, and my hat is off to them. But I still believe that Chicago is the better ball club."

From a baseball point of view the year of 1920 might best be described as "ominous." It was in 1920, after all, that the Black Sox scandal became known. When *The New York Times* wrote in its "Curves and Bingles" column on May 12 that "The white hose of the Chicago players is the same tint of white New York takes on three or four days after a snowstorm," one might think that they were on to something. But they weren't. In spite of occasional allegations, the scandal really didn't break until very late in the season. No, the White Sox hose was just plain dirty...the result of Chisox owner "Cheapskate Charlie" Comiskey being just plain too tight with the buck to have the team's duds properly laundered at all times. This lack of laundering had, as a matter of fact, been a problem since 1918, leading Sox players to sometimes refer to themselves, from 1918 on, as "the Black Sox."

And batting .303, his career high. Big games for Shano in 1920 included a two-for-five outing in a 7-3 win over the Browns on June 2; a contest vs. the Tigers on June 6 which saw Ty Cobb leave the game with an injured leg and Shano drive in the winning run in the eleventh

Mr. Owens Was Not Amused

A game not likely to be forgotten by Shano Collins – or anyone else who was on the premises – was a game that saw the White Sox take on Cleveland in Chicago on September 9, 1917. In the tenth inning of a 3-3 tie the Cleveland players protested a close call at third base. The players thought their runner, Jack Graney, was safe. The infield umpire, a Mr. Owens, thought otherwise. There followed ten minutes of arguing. When play was finally resumed the Indian players hurled their gloves in the air, and several of them rolled around in the infield dirt to show their displeasure. Then, after Chisox pitcher Dave Danforth had fanned leading off the White Sox tenth, Cleveland catcher Steve O'Neill threw the ball into center field. At that point Mr. Owens called the game, with the White Sox winning by the forfeit score of 9-0.

But if 1920 ended up being a bad year for the Sox – and for baseball – it was a good one for Shano. Veteran firstbaseman Chick Gandil had retired after the 1919 season, leaving the Sox high and dry with respect to the initial sack. Shano solved that by moving right in.

in a 7-6 Chicago victory; a four-for-five afternoon in a 10-3 trouncing of those same Tigers the next day; a two-for-five game in a 9-3 victory over the Senators on June 13; and a two-for-five performance in a 13-5 win over Detroit, yet again, on June 28.

OUTFIELD

Shano's bat remained hot as the summer progressed. He was two for four with a double as ace right-hander Urban "Red" Faber (who would finish the season at 23-13; go on to win 254 games lifetime, every one of them with the White Sox) shut down Detroit, 3-1, on July 27; and go two for four with a triple before 40,000 screaming fans at Comiskey Park in a 3-0 victory over the Yankees on August 1. The screaming, though, was mostly for the "mauling monarch" (as one paper called Babe Ruth as he was blasting his way to a 54-homer season). The fans wanted a Babe home run. They didn't get it.

Another personal favorite was no doubt a game also played against the Yankees: on August 26 the Sox beat ("massacred" is the word used by *The Times*) the New Yorkers by the score of 16-4. All Shano did was lash out two doubles and a triple – a bases-loaded triple, at that – during the course of the afternoon.

As September began all appeared relatively calm on the baseball front. In the American League the Indians and the White Sox were neck and neck, with the Yankees close behind. In the Senior Circuit, Brooklyn appeared to have the inside track on the flag. On September 5, however, it was announced that the Chicago chapter of the Baseball Writers of America – almost immediately to be replaced by a Chicago grand jury – was conducting an investigation regarding a reputedly fixed game between the Phillies and the Cubs just days earlier, on August 31. From there a finger of suspicion began, slowly but surely, to point back to the 1919 World Series. And certain White Sox members. Just which members was made public – very public: the scandal made headline news in most every paper in America – on September 28. Eight players – including the great Shoeless Joe Jackson and twenty-game winning pitchers Eddie Cicotte and Claude "Lefty" Williams – were indicted and immediately suspended.

That Shano was not one of the conspirators came as no surprise. While almost certainly also disgusted with the frugality of Charlie Comiskey, taking part in a fix was just not something the New Englander would do. As sportswriter Dan Daniel would write in his syndicated column, Daniel's Dope, "When the Black Sox got together to throw the world series to the Cincinnati Reds they did not bother taking Shano into their ring. They knew it would be dangerous to approach Shano. He would have sent the plot kicking."

With half their infield and two-thirds of their outfield suddenly "retired," the White Sox had a problem: how to finish the season. They were, after all, still in a three-games-to-go pennant race with the Indians. The Yankees – out of the race – actually stood up and offered Charlie Comiskey his choice of any and all Yankee players. "Our entire club is placed at your disposal," wired New York owners Jacob Ruppert and T.L. Huston. Needless to say, it didn't happen: the Babe didn't don an extra-large White Sox uniform. Nor did Wally Pipp or Bob Meusel or any other Yankee. No, instead Chicago manager Kid Gleason put together a patchwork squad of "Clean Sox" (as they were dubbed by the press). And these Patchworkers did their best. But they dropped two of the three remaining games, all versus the Browns, to finish in second. In this new squad's first and last win, a 10-7 slugfest over the Browns on October 1, Shano tore into the ball for four hits in five at-bats, with one of the four a triple. Call it good hitting. Or call it good therapy. It was probably both.

With his only .300-plus season, 1920, largely lost in the haze of the Black Sox, Shano was ready for a change. He got it. On March 4, 1921 Shano and teammate Nemo Leibold were traded to the Red Sox for longtime Boston mainstay Harry Hooper. It made sense. Red Sox proprietor Harry Frazee – as in "Rape of the Red Sox" Harry Frazee – was looking for ways to further trim his club's costs – while Hooper was holding out for $15,000: big bucks in 1921 – and White Sox owner Charlie Comiskey was looking to present a new team/new face in an attempt to wipe away the tarnish of the Black Sox. One very big plus for Shano: he got to play next door to where he grew up. Put another way: while Shano was going from one sinking ship (the White Sox would not finish higher than fifth for the next 15 years) to another sinking ship (the Red Sox would not finish higher than fifth for the next 13 years), at least he was close to family, friends, and the old neighborhood.

Six weeks later Shano was in a Boston uniform and in the Boston lineup as the Red Sox opened their season, April 13, against Washington in Washington. On hand to throw out the first pitch was president Warren G. Harding. Also on hand, but with no pitching duties involved, was Mrs. Harding, General John "Black Jack" Pershing, and American League president Ban Johnson. After the various and sundry ceremonies it was downhill quickly for the home team. Washington ace Walter Johnson gave way in the fifth after being hit hard. Shano, back in the outfield and playing center, hit a long triple in three trips to the plate. Final score: Boston 6, Washington, 3.

Three days later, Shano hit another triple in a two-for-four outing against those same Senators. This time it was Boston 8, and the Senators, 3. From Washington, the Sox moved on to New York and the Yankees. As *The New York Times* rather gracefully wrote: "The Red Sox of championship days have been gradually passing out of Boston uniforms, and the aggregation which took the field against the Huggins (Ed. note: Miller Huggins was the Yankee manager) maulers yesterday carried only one reminder of the big days in the Hub. That was (longtime Sox shortstop) Everett Scott." As for the game, ex-Sox submariner Carl Mays proved too much for the new Boston "aggregation," winning 4-0. Of note is that *The Times* wrote that Shano "made a remarkable catch near the pansy beds in deep centre field," cutting off what would have been two more New York runs. That same week, on April 25, Shano made a marvelous throw to cut down Jimmy Dykes at the plate and save a 3-2 win over the Athletics. On May 2, the outfielder drove in the winning run with a double in the eighth as the Sox beat New York, 2-1. Babe Ruth hit his sixth homer of the young season to account for the Yanks' only run.

Speaking of the Bambino, allow me to ask a question. Which baseball headline from May 4 holds the most intrigue?: "Senators Win In Tenth," "Tigers Claw The (White) Sox," or "Disturbs Babe's Bath." Number three certainly stands out in the crowd. It seems Mr. Ruth was at Boston's Hotel Brunswick enjoying his morning bath while the Yankees were in town, when who should appear but one John J. Buckley, a constable representing the City of Boston. The good constable had in his hand a warrant for alleged failure on the part of Babe to pay Boston property tax on his automobile for both 1919 and 1920; a sum of $47.21. The Babe, "clad very much like a Roman Gladiator," per the wire service report, got himself more formally attired, drove to city hall with Mr. Buckley, and there took an oath that he had not been a Boston resident the two years in question. Babe, minus Mr. Buckley, then returned to the Brunswick, "presumably to finish his plunge," as the press playfully wrote.

Other noteworthy games in Shano's rookie year with the Red Sox include a strong three-for-four showing in a 16-8 romp over his old team, the White Sox, on May 13; a win over the World Champion Indians, June 6, with Shano going two for four and scoring the winning run in a 7-6 close contest; going two for four — while also lining into a triple play! – in a 7-3 victory over the Brownies on June 10; watching as

Babe Ruth's 25th homer of the season sailed overhead in a game versus the Yankees at Fenway Park on June 23 (Ed. note: no other player in either league would hit that many home runs in the entire season); a 1-0 win over the White Sox, July 19, with Shano's Texas Leaguer driving in the game's sole run; going two for five with a run scored in a 15-2 trouncing of the Browns in St. Louis on August 23 (a game in which Sox pitcher Bullet Joe Bush slammed out a single, double, and triple and drove in five runs); knocking in teammate Del Pratt with the winning tally in a 6-5 eleven-inning win over the White Sox, August 27; and watching as Babe Ruth's 52nd homer of the season sailed overhead in a game versus the Yankees at the Polo Grounds on September 7. Shano was no slouch in that game, either: he hit three straight doubles. Not surprisingly, though, it was the "Bambino Blast" that got the ink. Wrote *The Times*: "Ruth's homer caused a cloudburst of straw hats. No sooner had the ball nestled among the fans in the lower tier of the right field grand stand than the air was thick with slightly tarnished but still serviceable chapeaux. If," concluded the scribe, "the habit continues it will be ultra-fashionable for baseball fans to go about bareheaded."

Shano Collins was to spend three more seasons with the Hub Hose. With each passing year, though, he saw less playing time. In 1922, he enjoyed his last season as a more-or-less full time player, batting .271 over 135 games. The Sox finished last in the league. In 1923, Shano appeared in 97 games, batting a lowly .231.

Red Sox owner Bob Quinn with his new manager, spring, 1931.
Shano would not be smiling for long.

OUTFIELD

The Sox finished last in the league. In 1924, Shano, now 38, saw action in 88 games, batting a rejuvenated .292. The Sox finished seventh. After two games in 1925, Shano hung up his glove. The Sox, their talent sold and traded away, were going nowhere. It was time for Shano to move on.

On June 2, 1925, Shano obtained his release from the Red Sox to take a position as player/manager with Pittsfield in the Eastern League. "He will leave for Pittsfield today," wrote *Boston Globe* sports columnist James C. O'Leary, "and thousands of his admirers and well wishers hope he may some day come back to the majors as a manager." Thus began Shano's second baseball career, that of manager. Stops, after his first Pittsfield stint, included Des Moines in the Western League in 1926-1927; then back to Pittsfield, the city he called home for many years. After a year, 1928, with the Hillies it was back to Des Moines again. Then came Nashua in the New England League, followed by another stay in Iowa's capital city.

On December 1, 1930, Shano lived up to James C. O'Leary's well-wishes of five years earlier: he signed on to become manager of the Red Sox. Commented sportswriter Harold C. Burr of *The Brooklyn Eagle*: "The tall, lean and leathery Collins has undeniable qualifications for the heretofore thankless job. Shano has a quick brain, acts with precision and possesses the eye to pick a player." The only problem: the players Shano were presented with were mostly tail-end material. Perennial tail-end

material. The Red Sox had gone through six managers since 1920. None had produced a winner. Nor would Shano. Actually, though, the old outfielder produced a miracle of sorts in 1931: he guided the team to a sixth-place finish, the team's highest berth since Cranston-native Hugh Duffy had led the team – with Shano patrolling right field – to a fifth-place mark in 1921. In 1932 the team began absymally. Then, on June 5, cash-poor Sox management traded the team's leading moundsman, Danny MacFayden (see pages 90-97), to the Yankees. That was it for Shano. He resigned two weeks later.

Shano later did some scouting for the Tigers, managed Woonsocket in the New England League in 1934, and managed Pittsfield for a third stretch in 1942. After his retirement from baseball, he was employed as a painter at Boston's Kenmore Hotel. John "Shano" Collins died at his home in Newton on September 10, 1955.

Photo, 1972

P.S. Newton, Massachusetts' native Bob Gallagher (full name: Robert Collins Gallagher), who played some outfield for the Red Sox, Astros, and Mets, 1972-1975, is Shano Collins' grandson. Now a high school teacher in Santa Cruz, California, Bob is proud of following in his granddad's footsteps. "But I was a shadow of the ballplayer Shano was," he modestly adds.

77

John Walter "Johnny" Cooney

Rhode Island's contribution to our starting team is quite a contribution. Johnny Cooney played an even 20 years in the bigs. For the first ten he was primarily a southpaw moundsmen. Then, when his throwing arm failed to do what he wanted it to do, he became an outfielder for the Dodgers and Braves for the second ten. In between was a five-year stretch in the minors. Most amazing is that at age 39, in 1940, the Cranston native batted .318, good enough for third best in the National League. The next year, when he should have been playing slow-pitch softball, Johnny Cooney came through with a .319 mark, second only in the NL to Pistol Pete Reiser's .343. Our man was also a year-in and year-out much-applauded defensive ace as well.

John Walter "Johnny" Cooney was born in Cranston, Rhode Island on March 18, 1901. His father, James Joseph "Jimmy" Cooney, and his older brother, James Edward "Jimmy" Cooney, had both played in the major leagues. Baseball was never a stranger to young Johnny. And, since he grew up before the regimented days of Little League, the budding ballplayer was out there with bat and glove just about every day from April until October. He was a left-handed thrower (who batted righty, a rather rare combination) and a mighty good one, starring in amateur ball in and around Cranston from his days at Highland Park High School on.

In 1920, Johnny graduated to semi-pro, twirling for the American Thread Company team out of Willimantic, Connecticut. Johnny's initial break came later that same 1920 season when the Thread Makers played an exhibition game against the Braves, and who should hold the Boston nine to just six hits but young Johnny. There followed a perfect game against the Rockville (Connecticut) league team and another no-hitter over an independent club from Bridgeport. At this point, the Red Sox almost – but not quite – signed the phenom. The story goes that the Sox offered the southpaw $500.00 to sign with them. But the $500.00 was to be in the form of a check, and Ed McGinley, Johnny's Willimantic manager and "agent," thought it should be in the form of cash. The deal was nixed. Next to come knocking were the Braves. They signed Johnny to a contract in the fall of 1920.

The southpaw spent the next season, 1921, with the Braves. He pitched little, appearing in only eight games, posting a 3.92 ERA and a record of 0-1. Most of 1922 was spent with New Haven in the (original) Eastern League. Johnny liked New Haven. He won 19 games, lost but three, and posted a sterling 1.92 ERA, second best in the loop as his team went on to cop the league championship.

New Haven was to be Johnny Cooney's high-water mark with respect to pitching. The hurler never really lived up to expectations thereafter. He did become known, though, for his "hesitation" pitch, a pitch he developed in the spring of 1923 after he noticed another pitcher slip on a wet mound. Johnny would rear back, halt, then fire away. This go/stop/go motion caught many a batter off-guard. Not surprisingly, the pitch was quite controversial: batters claimed the lefty was committing a balk every time he threw it. But umpires said no, it was legal. Hesitation pitch or no hesitation pitch, Johnny posted mediocre records in 1923 (3-5) and 1924 (8-9). His best major league season on the mound came in 1925 when the portsider was an even 14-14 with a 3.48 ERA as the Braves finished fifth. His 14 wins, in fact, tied Johnny with righty Larry Benton for most games won on the team. There was no tie, though, when it came to innings pitched: Johnny's 245⅔ were far and away the most on the Braves' staff. It may have been too much for Johnny's arm. He would never win – or lose, for that matter – in double figures in the majors again. In 1927 – after recording a mark of 3-3 in 1926 – Johnny sat out the season and underwent an operation to remove bone chips in his throwing arm. The operation caused his left arm to be two (or three or four, depending on which account you believe) inches shorter than his right one. Doctors said he would most likely never be able to use his left arm for much serious throwing again. Johnny just said

"Bosh," and set his sights on a comeback. And he did come back. Moreover, as difficult as it is to believe, he returned as a pitcher. But ho-hum marks in 1928-1930 convinced the Cranstonite that maybe he should give out-fielding a full-blown shot. He could, after all, always hit, plus he had played a fair amount of outfield (and some first base, too) throughout his career.

At the ripe old baseball age of 29, Johnny packed himself off to the minors in his come-back quest. First stop was the International League, where Johnny played for Jersey City and then Newark, compiling a combined average of .269 in 61 games in 1930. Next, in 1931, came Toledo in the American Association. There Johnny worked his average up to .289 in 117 games. Minor league stop number three was Indianapolis. He arrived planning to play one, maybe two, seasons. He ended up playing four, 1932-1935. Finally, however, after clouting a league-leading .371 in 1935, he got the call he was waiting for. It came from none other than Casey Stengel. Johnny and Casey had been teammates on the 1924-1925 Braves and Casey had been Johnny's manager at Toledo in 1932. Now he was at the helm of the Dodgers. And he wanted Johnny. The flychas-er from Cranston got into ten games for the Brooks in late 1935. That was nice. But 1936 was far nicer. Johnny was all smiles on April 7 as 1936 spring training wound down and Case announced to the press: "It appears that I have an outfield." A part of that outfield, of course, was Johnny. He'd earned a spot with strong

Johnny Cooney as he appeared with the Braves in 1925. It was his finest major league season on the mound and the man from the Ocean State was enjoying it.

defense plus a .356 mark in the Dodgers' exhibition games to that point.

On opening day, versus the arch-rival Giants, our favorite outfielder from Rhode Island held down the centerfield slot. Batting third in the order, Johnny went one for four as the Giants took the game, 8-5, before 56,000 at the Polo Grounds. In second game of the crosstown set he was 0 for 3, but bounced back with a solid two for four in the third and last tilt.

By looking through old box scores one gets a vision of Johnny's worth as a batsman. It takes comments by the media and other players, however, to get a view of his outfielding skills. Here's one such comment, from *The New York Times* of May 19, 1936: "Johnny Cooney came

through as usual with one difficult catch, racing into right center for (Kiki) Cuyler's fly in the sixth. In the two games against the Reds, Cooney has made eleven putouts and two assists, one to start a double play." Here's another: Burleigh Grimes, the venerable Dodger hurler (and future Hall of Famer), stated that Johnny was an outfielder who "has the brains to tell him where to go and the feet that carry him there." That's impressive stuff.

The 35-year old "rookie" went on to hit a solid .282 with 71 runs scored in 130 games for Brooklyn in 1936. An even more solid .293, in 120 games, followed in 1937. Meanwhile, Johnny's old pal, Casey Stengel, had been released by the Dodgers following the 1936 season. In 1938, Case signed on with the

OUTFIELD

Braves, and again he put in a call for Johnny: not only as a steady everyday ballplayer but as a no-nonsense example for the team's younger players. As an article in *The Sporting News* of November 25, 1940 would say so well: "(Cooney) is the game's oldest youngster – the man Casey Stengel holds up as a model for all his Bee (Braves) yearlings to copy in deportment, initiative and industry."

For Stengel and the Braves the Cranstonite hit .271 in 120 games in 1938, .274 in 118 games in 1939, and .318 in 108 games in 1940. It seemed that as he got older, Johnny got better. His .318 placed him third in the 1940 National League batting race, trailing only Debs Garms (.355) and Ernie Lombardi (.319). And he continued to be an acknowledged flyhawk par excellence. While often overlooked because he was (A) a singles hitter and (B) basically a quiet guy just doing his job, Johnny was not overlooked by Boston's baseball writers at the end of the 1940 season: they awarded him the coveted Walter Barnes Memorial Trophy as Boston's most valuable player. Move over Ted Williams, Jimmie Foxx, Dom DiMaggio, Joe Cronin, and Bobby Doerr.

In 1941, Johnny, playing some and sitting out some, didn't really get into high gear until April 21, when he went two for four with two runs scored and an RBI as veteran Wes Ferrell five-hit the Phillies at Braves Field. (Ed. note: it would be the last major-league victory for the longtime Indian – four twenty-game seasons – and Red Sox – two twenty-game seasons – star.). A little less than a week later, on April 27,

Johnny came through again against the Phils. He had three hits in five at-bats as Sailor Bill Posedel held Philadelphia in check, 8-3. Posedel also rapped out three hits in his own cause. Rounding out the month was the decision, on April 29, to again call the Braves the Braves. Gone were the Bees. (See page 94). Newly-elected team president Bob Quinn explained that "The boys (the players) don't like the nickname Bees and they insist that we again call ourselves the Braves." (Ed. note: one can only strongly suspect that the Bees would have remained the Bees if the team had been winning and/or piling in the fans. They were doing neither.).

The boys of Braves Field, though never in 1941's hotly contested pennant race, certainly had a hand in deciding it. A good example was when the highflying Cards arrived in Boston on May 6. The Cards, with an offense that featured Johnny Mize, Johnny Hopp, Enos Slaughter, Terry Moore, and Marty "The Octopus" Marion, were leading the league. Plus they'd won ten in a row; 13 in a row on the road. No matter. Johnny, batting second instead of his customary lead-off, was a major part of a surprise Boston victory. The outfielder went two for four with a run scored as the Braves took the contest, 5-4. The next day Johnny really got hot as the Stengeleers topped the Pirates, making a bid for a first-division berth, 7-6. Johnny's contribution: five hits – three of them doubles – in five at-bats with an RBI and two runs scored. Another Cooney batting barrage came on May 15. Again against

IT WAS A BASEBALL FAMILY

Johnny's dad, Jimmy (born in Cranston on July 9, 1865/died in Cranston on July 1, 1903), was the starting shortstop for Cap Anson's Chicago nine in 1890 and 1891, closing out a three-year major league career with Washington in 1892. Four of his sons – Johnny most definitely included – also enjoyed baseball success. Jimmy (born in Cranston on August 24, 1894/died in Warwick on August 7, 1991) held down short for the Red Sox, Giants, Cards, Cubs, Phils, and Braves. Harry, oldest of the four, played in both the New England and New York State Leagues. Frank enjoyed a ton of semi-pro in the Cranston/Providence area.

Johnny's older brother, Jimmy, played for six clubs in a seven-year career in the bigs. His best season was 1924, when he batted .295 with 20 doubles for the Cardinals. He is shown here as he appeared with the Braves in 1928.

the Cards, this time in St. Louis with the mercury reading a steamy 90°, our centerfielder rang up a double and three singles in five trips to the plate. Boston, with recently-acquired Lloyd Waner collecting three hits, won it by a score of 6-3, thereby dropping the Cards further behind the by-then front-running Dodgers.

It was probably more sentiment than sense, but old Case talked Braves' management into signing Paul Waner on May 24, allowing the storied Waner brothers, "Big Poison" and "Little Poison," to again play together. Casey wasted no time in positioning Lloyd and Paul together with Johnny in what could most certainly qualify as a veteran outfield. At least one scribe did his math and noted that when the three oldtimers took the field on May 25, their ages added up to a rather hefty total of 113.

The team's change in name did not cause the Braves to suddenly become a powerhouse. Sluggers they were not. Occasionally, though, the Braves' bats would go into overdrive. One such occasion was June 8 when, after losing the first game of a doubleheader against the Cubs, 5-1, Johnny and company rolled to a 13-1 lopsided win in the nightcap. The Braves big runs that game were Johnny (three for four with an RBI and a run scored), firstbaseman Ellsworth "Babe" Dahlgren (two for four with four RBIs and a run scored), secondbaseman Carvel "Bama" Rowell (two for five with three runs scored), and leftfielder Gene Moore (a home run and three runs scored). Even pitcher Al Javery (see page 111) joined in the onslaught:

he was one for four with an RBI and a pair of runs scored. Johnny and Javery, as a matter of fact, seemed to work well together. With the rookie from Worcester on the mound against Cincinnati on June 18, Johnny went two for four with an RBI and a run scored in a 4-2 Braves win. Johnny "Double No-Hit" Vander Meer took the loss for the defending World Champion Reds.

Nor were Johnny's defensive skills lessening as he steadily advanced toward birthday number 41. In a game against Bill Terry and his Giants on July 2, Johnny ate up a first inning smash off Mel Ott's always potent bat. Wrote *New York Times*' Boston correspondent Louis Effrat: "Ott smashed a screaming 400-foot drive to dead center, but Cooney, who improves with age, pulled it down, even while bouncing off the concrete wall. Ottey hasn't hit many balls harder than he did this one, but it was just a time at bat." The Braves went on to win, 5-4, with thirdsacker Sibby Sisti (three for four with an RBI and two runs scored) and firstbaseman Buddy Hassett (two for four with a run scored) the Braves' offensive heroes of the day. Worth noting is that when an announcement came over the loud-speaker that Joe DiMaggio had surpassed Wee Willie Keeler's record of hitting safely in 44 consecutive games, the crowd gave a vigorous cheer.

It was another win for Al Javery on July 3. The righty pitched a five-hitter versus the Phillies in Boston. Before a meager crowd of 1,003, the Braves won it by scoring three runs in the seventh on singles by Sibby Sisti, Johnny, an error, and a double by the Braves' leading power threat, outfielder Max West. Sisti and Johnny teamed up again to do a job on the Cubs, 7-2, on July 11. Sibby, who spent his entire 13-year major league career with the Braves, hammered three doubles and a single while Cranston's favorite centerfielder joined the fun with a double, two singles, and a sacrifice. Jim Tobin, who would win in double figures for the Braves in 1941, 1942, 1943, and 1944, gained the win.

In his esteemed Sports of the (New York) Times column of July 13, John Kieran gave his views on the state of baseball and its players. After discussing the likes of Ted Williams, Joe DiMaggio, Pete Reiser, and Johnny Mize, Mr. Kieran turned to Johnny Cooney. Here's what he had to say: "But the hitter to whom this awed onlooker doffs his chapeau is the aged – or ageless – Johnny Cooney of the Braves. This 40-year-oldster is in the upper class at bat and if there's a better fly-chaser in the league it must be Terry Moore of the Cardinals, eleven years Cooney's junior." Well-deserved praise, indeed.

On the thirteenth, the Braves topped the fourth-placed Reds in a thriller. Down 5-4 in the last of the ninth, the Bostonians scored twice off Cincinnati ace Paul Derringer when Johnny singled, Sibby Sisti walked, and then both scored on a double by Maxie West. The Braves then did it again to Derringer (a 20-game winner in four of his previous six seasons) and the Reds on August 2. With Paul Waner getting four hits, Sibby Sisti three, and

Johnny two, Boston took home the win, 6-1.

August also saw more praise from John Kieran. In listing the strong points of each major league club on the fourteenth, the noted columnist wrote: "The bright, particular star of the Braves this year has been an ancient gent, almost an antique, certainly a historical figure by this time. That's Johnny Cooney who is, at 40, one of the neatest hitters and smoothest outfielders in the league." Johnny must have had a sixth sense: the "ancient gent" went four for nine with two doubles and three RBIs in a twinbill against the Giants on the thirteenth, just about the time Kieran would have been putting the finishing touches on his next-day's column. As for the doubleheader, the Braves lost the opener but took the nightcap as Winchester-native Art Johnson held the New Yorkers to seven hits in a 3-1 win.

Another example of the Braves' involvement in the red-hot St. Louis vs. Brooklyn pennant battle of '41 came on August 10 when they knocked off the Dodgers, 4-1, with Johnny blasting a bases-loaded triple in the second. Tom Earley, a Roxbury native enjoying his best season in the six summers he would spend with the Braves, held the powerful Brooks to seven hits, while Lowell's Skippy Roberge (see page 61) aided the Braves' cause with a double, a run scored, and an RBI. Generally, though, it was the boys of Brooklyn who did the winning. With a line-up that included Dixie Walker, Billy Herman, Dolf Camilli, Pee Wee Reese, Joe Medwick, Cookie Lavagetto, and Pete Reiser, there weren't many teams that could keep up with Leo Durocher's bunch. The sole exception was the Cardinals. And it was St. Louis and Brooklyn right down to the wire.

Johnny, meanwhile, went on a hitting spree. Through the games of August 2, the

ers. A four-for-five outing against the feeble Phillies on September 7 helped. So did a three-for-four afternoon against the Cubs on September 14.

Mostly, though, September of 1941 – the

NOT A SLUGGER

Johnny was not a slugger. It took him 15 seasons and over 2300 at-bats before he hit his first fourbagger. The momentous event came to pass in a game against the Giants at the Polo Grounds on September 24, 1939 off Giant hurler Harry "Gunboat" Gumbert. Johnny's drive was a high fly right down the left-field line. What's more amazing, perhaps, is that the very next day Johnny hit another homer. Against the same team in the same park. That one, though, was off Bill Lohrman and was a shot down the right-field line. Johnny would then play an additional five seasons without ever hitting another circuit clout. (A postscript to Johnny's first roundtripper came in a December 2002 letter to me from long-time Brave infielder Sibby Sisti. Sibby, in his first season with the Braves in 1939, well recalls Johnny's homer. "We were," he remembers, "so shocked that we pulled the silent act on him and no one congratulated him or said anything for five minutes.").

Boston star was tagging the ball at a .307 clip. He stood eighteenth in the National League. Over the next eight weeks, however, the outfielder moved up to .319, surpassing Johnny Hopp, Johnny Mize, Stan Hack, Arky Vaughan, Joe Medwick, and Enos Slaughter, among others.

last September before Pearl Harbor – focused on the Cardinal-Dodger race. The Cards took two from the Braves in St. Louis on the seventeenth. Playing his first major league game that day was a 20-year old outfielder the Cards had just called up from Rochester. His name was

Johnny was appointed acting manager of the Braves when Billy Southworth took ill in August of 1949. Here he is getting the scoop from his wife Alice at Braves Field in his second week on the job.

OUTFIELD

Stan Musial. And he cracked out a double and a single to help the Cardinals climb to within a game of Brooklyn. The next day, the eighteenth, Musial was again in the line-up. But to no avail. The Braves, behind the strong pitching of Manny Salvo, beat St. Louis, 4-1. Johnny went two for four with a run scored as the Cards failed to gain on the Dodgers, who also lost, 6-5, to the Pirates.

The Dodgers put the race to bed on September 24 and 25 by taking back-to-back games from, as you might guess, the Braves. Dixie Walker's bases-loaded triple and the pitching of Kirby Higbe did the job for Brooklyn on the first day, while Whitlow Wyatt's 22nd win, a 6-0 shutout, did the trick on the second. The Dodgers had won their first flag since 1920.

The season of 1941 was over. It was a splendid season for Brooklyn. And for Johnny Cooney. His .319 was bettered by only the wondrous – while healthy – Pete Reiser. Pistol Pete batted .343. Over in the Junior Circuit, a left-fielder named Ted William led all hitters with a tidy .406 mark. "The Splendid Splinter" was trailed by the Senators' Cecil Travis at .359 and the Yankees' Joe DiMaggio at .357.

Johnny played three more seasons in the majors. It was mostly bits and pieces stuff, though, as age was finally catching up with him. He appeared in 74 games for the Braves in 1942, sinking to .207. He then moved back to Brooklyn where he hit .206 in 37 games, primarily as a pinchhitter. After beginning the season of 1944 with the Dodgers, Johnny found himself in a Yankee uniform. He totaled an even .333 for the season, but it was in a mere 17 games. Johnny's lifetime major league numbers: 965 hits in 3372 at-bats over 20 seasons for a crisp .286 average.

At age 43, Mr. Cranston Baseball bowed out of the major leagues as a player. He was not yet ready to hang up his bat and glove, however. The flyhawk did some outfielding for Toronto, then in the International League, and for Kansas City (where he hit .343 in 1945), then in the American Association. In December of 1946, Johnny was again signed by the Braves. Not to play, but to coach. And, as manager Billy Southworth's right-hand man, he was a major factor in the success of the '48 Braves. In August of 1949, Johnny was pressed into service as the acting Braves' manager, filling in for the rest of the season for the mentally-drained Southworth. Johnny remained with the Braves through 1955. Later, beginning in 1957, our man served as batting coach for the White Sox. With Chicago, the old vet was instrumental in the winning ways of the 1959 Go Go Sox. He retired from the White Sox – and from baseball – in 1965.

Just as he had played well, Johnny had invested well. This was especially true with respect to Florida real estate, and Johnny lived comfortably in Sarasota after his baseball days had run their long course. He died in Sarasota Memorial Hospital in Sarasota on July 8, 1986.

PATRICK JOSEPH "PAT"/ "DOC" CARNEY

– no photo available – was born in Holyoke, Massachusetts on August 7, 1876, and died in Worcester, Massachusetts on January 9, 1953. Was a fleet-of-foot outfielder for Holy Cross and then, from 1901-1904, the Beaneaters (Braves). Liked to take the mound at times, too. Although far from a star at either position, he did bat a first-rate .270 with 27 stolen bases in 137 games in 1902. Pitching-wise his best season was 1903 when he won four games while losing five. Lived up to nickname of "Doc" by later becoming a practicing physician. Lifetime is .247 in 338 games.

JOSEPH ALOYSIUS "JOE"/ "JOEY" CONNOLLY,

shown here in a pair of circa 1914 photos, was born in North Smithfield, Rhode Island on February 12, 1888 and died in North Smithfield, Rhode Island on September 1 1943. Started his career as a pitcher for St. Mary's School in Pawtucket. Then, still a moundsman, starred in semi-pro ball in Woonsocket area. Discovered by local scout and sent to Little Rock in the Southern Association, 1908. Played for Little Rock, Zanesville (Ohio), Terre Haute (Indiana), and Montreal (then in International League), 1908-1912. While at Zanesville, 1910, injured arm pitching

SIMON "SI" ROSENTHAL

– no photo available – was born in Boston on November 13, 1903 and died in Boston on April 7, 1969. Signed off Boston sandlots at age 17, in 1920. Saw action with San Antonio, Pittsfield, and Albany before got chance with Red Sox, 1925. Hit .264 in 19 games for Sox, 1925. Enjoyed best – and last – season in majors, 1926, when batted .267 in 104 games for Sox. Hampered by foot injury, still went on to play minor-league ball for host of clubs, including Louisville, Chattanooga, Dallas, Nashville, Galveston, Mobile, Quincy, and, finally, Peoria. Was decorated hero in WWII.

both ends of a doubleheader, and became an outfielder from then on. Led Central League with mark of .355 for Terre Haute, 1911. Hit .316 for Montreal, 1912. Signed by Braves, 1913, and hit a solid .281, second-highest mark on club. Was vital part of Braves' offense in their spectacular come-from-last-place "Miracle Braves" season of 1914, hitting .306 (the only regular on team to hit .300), stealing a dozen bases, and playing a strong left field. And his nine home runs were among league leaders, as were his 28 doubles and .494 slugging average. Fell off slightly to a .298 average in 1915 (still tops on the team); then really dipped, with an injured leg, to .227 in 62 games, 1916. Asked by club management to take a cut in his $2,400 salary for 1917, Joe said

"nope," preferring to return to the family farm in North Smithfield. Stayed close to the farm the remainder of his life, finding time to also serve as an investigator for the Rhode Island State Board of Milk Control, as well as both state assemblyman and state senator. Lifetime is .288 in 412 games.

Joe Connolly was the sole regular player on the 1914 "Miracle Braves" to bat over .300. Next, after Joey's .306, came firstbaseman Butch Schmidt's .285 and future Hall-of-Famer and second baseman Johnny Evers' .279.

Daniel Knowles "Danny"/ "Deacon Danny" MacFayden

Danny MacFayden didn't look like your average ballplayer. One of the very first bespectacled professional athletes, "Deacon Danny" had the appearance, per noted sportswriter Tom Meany, of "a Harvard botany professor." But Danny had a curve that veteran catcher (19 years in the bigs) Al Lopez said made him the best curveball pitcher he ever caught. Strangely, though, Danny MacFayden was a pitcher who performed better for second-division clubs, especially second-division Boston clubs. With the Red Sox (1926-1932) and the Braves (1935-1939 and 1943) he was good, sometimes great. With the powerhouse Yankees (1932-1934) he was mediocre. When his 17-year major league career came to an end, the former moundsman accepted a position as baseball coach at Bowdoin College. He would remain in that capacity from 1946 until 1970.

Daniel Knowles "Danny" MacFayden was born in North Truro, near the tip of Cape Cod, Massachusetts, on June 10, 1905. He grew up in Somerville and was, in fact, a teammate of future major leaguers Francis "Shanty" Hogan (see pages 96-97 and 114-115), and Haskell Billings (who would do some pitching for the Tigers in the late 1920s) at Somerville High. A scholar/athlete, Danny was urged by his mother to go to Dartmouth. Danny much preferred, however, baseball over academia. He was a strong hitter in high school, but come graduation he found himself taking the mound in the semi-pro leagues that abounded in the Boston/Cape Cod area. He hurled for Osterville in 1923 and 1924, and Falmouth in 1925. He was spotted and signed by the Red Sox in 1926. Brought up immediately to the parent club, Danny saw little action in 1926. He was, though, forever asking questions and taking notes. It was a practice that would serve him in good stead all through his long career, both in pitching and coaching.

Danny spent six full seasons with the Red Sox, each season winning more games than the previous one. He notched no wins (vs. one loss) in 1926; five wins (vs. eight losses) in 1927; nine wins (vs. 15 losses) in 1928; ten wins (vs. 18 losses) in 1929; eleven wins (vs. 14 losses) in 1930; and 16 wins (vs. twelve losses) in 1931. If these records don't sound bedazzling, it's because Danny was pitching for the Sox during their Dark Ages. Except for 1931, Boston was mired deep in last place for all the MacFayden years. In 1931, they "leaped" up to number six on the American League ladder

PITCHER

Danny's mother wanted Danny to go to Dartmouth. Danny wanted to play pro ball. Guess who won.

Circa 1930 photo

with a record of 62-90 and with Danny accounting for fully twenty-five percent of the team's total win count.

Danny's best year with the Sox, 1931, started slowly, but once in the groove he pretty much remained in the groove. Games of note that winning year include a five-hit win over the Browns, 6-3, in Fenway Park on June 7; a game against Detroit on June 22 in which Danny allowed twelve hits but just two runs in going the route for a 7-2 victory; and a six-hitter in a 7-1 win over the White Sox in Chicago, June 30. Then there was his gem against the Yankees, July 5, going eleven innings as the Sox took it 6-3. The headline in *The New York Times* read: "MacFayden Proves Puzzle," continuing, "The Yankees' victory wave stumbled over a slim, shrewd Boston ace named Danny MacFayden at the Stadium yesterday." Not only did Deacon Danny top the Bombers, he completely shut down the booming bats of both Ruth and Gehrig. *The Times* again: "The crowd of 12,000 expected to see Ruth and Gehrig (tied for the league lead with twenty roundtrippers apiece) continue their homer-shooting duel, but to its astonishment the little Red Sox moundsman kept them from getting even a single." There followed an eight-hitter over the Indians, 4-1, on July 18 with Mac striking out Willie Kamm and future Hall-of-Famer Earl Averill with the bases loaded in the seventh; a 1-0 whitewash of Red Faber and the White Sox, August 15 (*The Times* noted that the Chisox had nine hits but "whenever a threat developed the Red Sox hurler put on the pressure and bowled over Chicago batsmen with flaw-

Circa 1931 photo

Rightfielder Earl Webb played two complete seasons for the Red Sox. In one of those seasons, 1931, he slammed out a monumental 67 doubles. It was the single-season major league record then. It's the single-season major league record now.

less skill."); a three-hitter over the Tigers, 5-0, on September 11; a ten-inning thriller, 3-2, again over the White Sox (with Danny scoring the winning tally), September 15; and another thriller, 2-1, over Cleveland at Fenway on September 19. By finishing strong, Danny, manager Shano Collins (see pages 68-77), and the team had done it: they'd climbed out of the cellar for the first time in seven years. In fact, they finished sixth, ahead of Detroit and Chicago. In his season-end wrap-up, *Times* sportswriter John Kieran noted in his "Sports of the Times" column that "Shano Collins had some very good pitching, especially from Danny MacFayden." Indeed, Danny's sixteen wins placed him in a tie for seventh most wins in the league (with Lefty Grove's truly amazing 31-4 leading the pack).

In 1932, Danny began poorly. Very poorly. He lost ten of his first eleven decisions. Then, in spite of the poor start, the almost inevitable happened. The Yankees saw a player they liked. He was wearing a Red Sox uniform. The Yankees made an offer. Voila: the player was wearing a Yankee uniform. On June 5, 1932, Danny became a Yankee. To get him, New York parted with two pretty fair pitchers, Ivy Andrews and Hank Johnson, as well as $50,000. Senators' owner Clark Griffith, also desirous of Danny's right arm, had offered Buddy Myer (who would win the AL batting championship in 1935 with a .349 mark), an unnamed pitcher, and $55,000. But once again it was the Boston-to-New York pipeline that prevailed. So Danny followed in the footsteps

of Babe Ruth, Waite Hoyt, Carl Mays, Herb Pennock, and Red Ruffing. All went from the Sox to the Yanks. And all went on to greatness. Not Danny, though. The Pride of Somerville never became the Pride of the Bronx. With the Yankees he was 7-5 for the remainder of 1932. Then came a 3-2 mark (with an ERA of 5.88) in 1933 and a 4-3 mark (with an ERA of 4.50) in 1934. Certainly nothing to write about to the folks back home in the Bay State.

What happened? It's unlikely that Mac felt overawed by Ruth, Gehrig, Chapman, and company. In fact, early-on in his Yankee days the Somerville Scot commented how much he liked the big crowds and winning ways. Danny's own answer – as to why he was ineffective – was lack of work. He was, he explained, primarily a curve-ball pitcher, and a curve-ball pitcher must have pinpoint control in order to be effective. Without work he won't have that control. It's also possible that Mac was a pitcher who worked better with a low pressure (translate: second division) club than with a pennant contender. One sportswriter would, after Danny had clicked with the Braves in 1936, call him an example of being "majestic in mediocrity." Whatever the case, Danny was far more effective in a Boston uniform that a New York uniform.

Maybe he just liked Boston better.

On November 13, 1934, Danny was sold to the Cincinnati Reds for an undisclosed amount of cash. He was not to remain a Redleg for long. After a 1-2 record in seven games Danny was sold, again for an undisclosed amount of cash, back home to Massachusetts. This time to the Braves. It took part of the summer of 1935 – Danny was but 5-13 in his debut season with the Braves – but then the elixir of pitching in the Hub again came bubbling through. Not counting his debut year, Danny pitched in direct contrast to his Red Sox seasons: he won fewer games each successive year. He began with a hefty 17 victories in 1936 and worked his way south to eight wins in 1939. His 17 in 1936 was most impressive. More so was his ERA of 2.87. Only the great "King Carl" Hubbell of the Giants had a lower mark, 2.31. Dizzy Dean came in third at 3.17.

With Danny leading the way, the Braves were an almost-respectable 71-83 in 1936, good enough for a lock on sixth place. It may also have helped that the Braves sported a new nickname in 1936. The team was now known as the "Bees." An obvious attempt to draw more fans, the new moniker impressed some more than others. *New York Times* writer John Drebinger commented that "Known as the Braves, the club at least had a formidable name. Now, with practically all of the old-time sting removed, they are being called the Bees." (Ed. note: the team would go back to being the Braves in 1941.).

Some of Danny's more memorable outings that season of 1936 included a five-hit 3-1 victory over his former team, the Reds, in Cincinnati on April 30; a masterful three-hit shutout over Paul "Daffy" Dean on May 5 in which, per the Associated Press, "Danny MacFayden held the Cardinals in almost com-

Circa 1932 photo

When Danny was traded from the Red Sox to the Yankees in June of 1932 big things were expected of him. It was, after all, difficult not to win when you had Lou Gehrig, Ben Chapman, Tony Lazzeri, Earle Combs, Bill Dickey, and the Bambino on your side.

plete subjection" as Boston won, 1-0 (and this was the Cardinals of Joe Medwick, Frankie Frisch, Johnny Mize, Terry Moore, and Pepper Martin); a fourteen-hitter (yes, a fourteen-hitter) in which Danny bore down in lots of tough spots in besting the Reds again, 8-3, on June 7; yet another triumph over the Reds, 4-1, on July 10; a 4-1 win over the Pirates at Braves Field on July 29; and a 3-2 victory over the Cardinals, July 25, in which Tony Cuccinello's three-run homer for the Bees topped Johnny Mize's two-run shot for the Cards, and Danny stopped a Joe Medwick 21-game hitting streak.

Danny was primarily a starting pitcher. And what he started he generally finished as well. Only Dizzy Dean, Carl Hubbell, and the Dodgers' Van Lingle Mungo had more complete games than Danny's 21 in 1936. However, the righthander worked in relief from time to time, too. On May 13, he took over for starter John Lanning against the Pirates in the fifth inning and remained on the mound through the tenth, when he scored the winning run after drawing a pass. Two and a half weeks later, on May 31, the scenario was much the same as Danny went into the game in the eighth in relief of Bees' starter Ray Benge; went on to score the winning run in the eleventh after singling to lead off the inning. Boston rightfielder Wally Berger hit his fifth homer of the season in the fourth. The Braves' only real long ball threat, Berger had taken NL home run honors with 34 in 1935, and would go on to clout a total of 25 in 1936.

Danny's winning ways continued in the season's second half. Victories included a 4-3 outing over the first-place Cubs before a Braves Field crowd of 26,000 on August 2; and a 4-2 win over Brooklyn ace Van Lingle Mungo,

IN CASE YOUR HEARING IS AS BAD

Normally on the mild-mannered side, Danny MacFayden is yet recalled in baseball lore and legend for one time he wasn't. He was on the mound for the Pirates against the Phillies during the season of 1940. The bases were loaded, and the count was three and two to the Phillie batter, Bobby Bragan. Danny threw one right down the pipe. It looked perfect. Bill Klem, umpiring behind the plate, however, called "Ball four." Danny was livid. He was off the hill and at Klem in a flash. Offering the umpire his glasses, Danny shouted, "You need these worse than I do." With that, Klem banished Danny from the game. Danny protested, saying the punishment was too severe for the crime. Klem, though, said he bounced Danny because the pitcher had shouted, allowing the fans to hear what he'd said. To which Danny replied, "I shouted for your benefit...in case your hearing is as bad as your eyesight."

Only Carl "The Meal Ticket" Hubbell had a lower earned run average than Danny MacFayden in the National League in 1936. Hubbell's was 2.31, while Danny's was 2.87. No one else in the league – and that includes the likes of Dizzy and Daffy Dean, Big Bill Lee, Paul Derringer, Claude Passeau, Lon Warneke, and Bucky Walters – was under 3.00.

Wheaties ad, 1936

PITCHER

August 8. Although certainly not in the pennant race, a tight three-way contest between the Cubbies, Cardinals, and Giants, Danny and the Bees were very much involved in influencing it. An outstanding example was a gem of a pitchers' duel in St. Louis on August 27 between MacFayden and the Cards' Roy Parmelee. Parmelee had a no-hitter until the eighth; a shutout until the tenth, when Bees' thirdbaseman Joe Coscarart slammed a triple to score Tony Cuccinello from second. Danny went all the way, allowing the powerful Cards but five safeties. Showing no favorites, the Bees swept a twinbill from Mel Ott, Bill Terry, Travis Jackson and the Giants on September 5. Danny beat Freddie Fitzsimmons, 6-2, in the opener while Giant-castoff Jim Chaplin beat Hal Schumacher, 7-3, in the nightcap. A Polo Grounds' crowd of 38,000 was not pleased. A game that Danny should have won, but didn't, was a contest against the Cardinals on September 9. Both teams scored in the first inning, then remained runless for the next fourteen. And, in those days before pitch counts, both Danny and the Cards' Jim Winford just kept on pitching. St. Louis shortstop Leo Durocher collected five hits, including the game-winner in the 15th. Two final wins rounded out Danny's 17-win season. The first was a six-hit 6-1 triumph over the Reds on September 13. The second came over the Phillies, 5-3, on September 20th, with Danny singling to start the game-winning rally in the fifth. The Giants, incidentally, took the 1936 pennant, then went on to be hammered four games to two by a Yankee team that included Lou Gehrig, Bill Dickey, George "Twinkletoes" Selkirk, Tony Lazzeri, (Penacook, New Hampshire-native) Red Rolfe, and a rookie named Joe DiMaggio.

Following his big season of 1936, Mac had two fourteen-game winning seasons in a row. In both seasons, his ERA, 2.93 in 1937 and 2.95 in 1938, was among the league's lowest. In 1939, he slipped to a 3.90 ERA, and a disappointing record of 8-14. The Bees' braintrust, which included a relatively young Casey Stengel as manager, decided it was time for a parting of the ways. On December 8, 1939, Danny was traded to the Pirates for pitcher Bill Swift and cash. After one season, 1940, in which he was 5-4 with a 3.55 ERA, Danny was released. Pirate president Bill Benswanger noted that Bucs' manager Frankie Frisch wanted to rebuild the team with youth. At age 36, Danny found himself with the Washington Senators, for whom he was 0-1 with a sky-high ERA of 10.29 in 1941. That would have been it but for World War II creating a need for able-bodied/non-draftable players. Danny qualified on both counts. The Braves picked him up in 1943. He went 2-1 that season before retiring as an active player for good.

Always the New Englander, the old curveballer moved to Brunswick, Maine, accepting an offer to coach the Bowdoin College nine. That he did and did well for 24 seasons, from 1946 to 1970. He also coached some hockey for Bowdoin, too. Danny MacFayden died in Brunswick on August 26, 1972.

Somerville High's 1925 baseball team, as pictured in the school yearbook, **The Radiator.** *That's Shanty Hogan circled in the middle back row; and Danny MacFayden circled second-from-the-right back row (and Haskell Billings circled far right back row). The team's nickname was the Highlanders (Somerville High School sits on Highland Avenue). And, yes, they were good. As of the date that the 1925 yearbook went to press the team was 14-0 and had outscored their opponents 126-31.*

SOMERVILLE HIGH

Senior year, 1925, yearbook photo of Danny. His nickname was "Dan." His class quote: "Gentleman, scholar, heartbreaker, athlete."

Senior year, 1925, yearbook photo of Shanty. Our catcher-to-be was then nick-named "Gimpty." His class quote: "A great and mighty man is he."

As we pause after paying tribute to our right-handed moundsman – a graduate of Somerville High – before we move on to pay tribute, a few pages further along, to our catcher – a graduate of Somerville High – let us pay tribute to Somerville High. A rather remarkable 30% of our starting team graduated from SHS. In addition to pitcher Danny MacFayden and catcher Francis "Shanty" Hogan, we have secondbaseman Horace "Hod" Ford (see pages 30-35), a 1915 grad. Of further note is that one other player pictured here also went on to spend some time in a major league uniform. That's Haskell Billings. Haskell, standing tall to the far right in the back row of the photo included here, never became a household word...but he did put in three seasons, 1927-1929, as a pitcher for the Tigers, compiling a lifetime 10-15 mark.

There have been, as well, at least a dozen more major leaguers through the years who have a close connection with Somerville.

These include Arthur "Skinny" Graham (who did some outfielding for the Red Sox in 1934-1935), Art Mahan (who hit .244 in 145 games at first for the Phils in 1940), and Gil Whitehouse (who saw limited action with the Braves in 1912 and with Newark in the Federal League in 1915).

Last of all, and a man definitely not to be overlooked, is Harold "Pie" Traynor. The Hall of Fame thirdbaseman was not born in the City of Hills. Nor did he attend Somerville High. But he did spend most of his formative years in Somerville and reputedly earned his distinctive nickname from the fondness for pie he displayed while growing up there.

I asked Jerry Knight, present-day Athletic Director at Somerville High, how come his area produced so many ballplayers good enough to make it to the majors. He laughed and said, "Luck." But he then quickly added that "Somerville was always a baseball (and basketball) town."

George Albert "Lefty" Tyler

Considered one of the National League's stellar left-handed pitchers of his day, George "Lefty" Tyler played a key role in the greatest comeback in major league history, the last-place-to-first-place saga of the 1914 "Miracle" Boston Braves. He also – pitching for the opposing Chicago Cubs – appeared in three games in the last World Series ever won by the Red Sox...the Series of 1918.

On July 14, 1914 a record heat wave killed four persons in St. Louis. The mayor of Terre Haute, Indiana was held in contempt by the federal government for interfering with a federal sewerage project in his fair city. Department store magnate John Wanamaker celebrated his seventy-sixth birthday. The New York, New Haven & Hartford Railway advertised the White Mountains as possessing "Air that is a joy and a tonic." And the Boston Braves were seemingly securely ensconced in last place in the National League. That they were in last was not too awfully surprising: the Braves had finished at the bottom in 1912 and a weak fifth in 1913.

Then the completely unexpected happened. The Braves started to win. And win. And win. There was no stopping them. And one of the reasons why was George Albert "Lefty" Tyler.

Born in Derry, New Hampshire on December 14, 1889, "Lefty" – as he was generally called – was signed by Lowell in the old New England League in 1909 after playing some serious semi-pro ball in and around Derry and attending St. Anselm College in Manchester. The Braves purchased Lefty's contract from Lowell in July of 1910 and saw the portsider post marks of 0-0 in 1910, 7-10 in 1911, 12-22 in 1912, and 16-17 (with a league-leading 28 complete games) in 1913.

Then came 1914. As with the rest of the team, Lefty started on the slow side. As of July 11, he was a mediocre 6-8. He would, however, go on to win ten more games that marvelous season, and was especially effective in July and August as the Braves passed team after team in their heady climb up the National League ladder. Games in which Lefty was at his very best included July 20, when he held the Pirates to four hits in a 1-0 win; July 23, when he again shut out the Bucs, this time 2-0; August 3, when the southpaw bested the Cards on a 1-0, three-hit shutout (with Lefty himself scoring the game's only run); August 19, when Lefty held the Reds to eight hits in a 3-2 squeaker; and August 30, when he held St. Louis to but one hit in a 2-0 victory. "For a time it seemed that George had decided to abolish hits altogether," wrote *The New York Times* in describing the one-hitter.

Lefty's finest outing of 1914 – and certainly

PITCHER

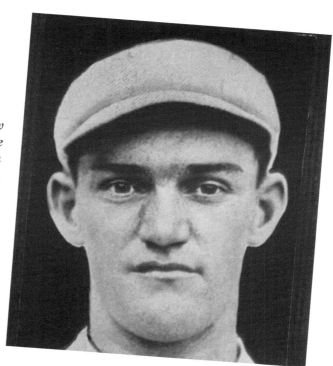

Signed by Lowell in the New England League in 1909, George "Lefty" Tyler joined the Braves a year later and went on to win in double figures eight times in a twelve-year major league career.

Circa 1912 photo

the most highly charged – was the game of August 15, matching first-place New York and second-place Boston. *The Times* labeled the contest as "one of the most brilliant struggles ever staged at the historic Polo Grounds, pitting the great Christy Mathewson versus the 'little' (Ed. note: actually, records list Lefty as being six feet tall.) George Tyler. Pitcher after pitcher of the Giants staff," continued *The Times* in the dramatic style of the period, "had been swept before the Boston avalanche in the previous games of the series, until only Mathewson remained to stem the tide."

Well, the tide remained unstemmed. For nine full innings the two moundsmen matched each other in an almost pitch-by-pitch duel. In the tenth, however, veteran Braves' catcher Hank Gowdy tripled in one run and then scored himself on a Matty wild pitch. Lefty beat Matty, 2-0…and the Braves marched on.

During their amazing run the Braves were called, by the media, "rejuvenated," "galloping," "rampaging," and "wonderful." They were, indeed, all of those. It paid off on September 2 when Boston took over the league's top spot as John McGraw and his Giants lost to Brooklyn, 6-2, while the Bostonians swept a twinbill from the Phils, 7-5 and 12-3, in Philadelphia. Back in Boston, at Fenway Park, even Red Sox fans applauded the Braves' achievement. "At the announcement (that the Braves had taken over first place), the crowd stood up and cheered long and lustily," penned *The Times'* Red Sox correspondent, continuing, "It was an American League crowd, but every man and woman in the place

101

Lefty, shown here in a 1914 photo, was one of the Miracle Braves' "Big Three," teaming up with Dick Rudolph and Bill James to account for 69 of the Braves' 94 wins.

was a Brave rooter." (Ed. note: with a little luck and a few more wins, the Red Sox, who came in second behind Connie Mack's Philadelphia Athletics, could have met the Braves in a 1914 subway series. Wouldn't *that* have given Boston's fans something to cheer about!).

By season's end, Boston manager George Stallings (dubbed "The Miracle Man") and his troupe were well atop the Senior Circuit. Their winning ingredients: superb pitching, the backstopping of Hank Gowdy, the infield play of sparkplug Walter "Rabbit" Maranville (a native of Springfield, Massachusetts) and Johnny "The Crab" Evers, and the bat of left-fielder Joe Connolly (also a New Englander: see pages 88-89), who enjoyed a career year and was the team's only .300 hitter, at .306, while also slugging out a then-impressive nine home runs.

In spite of their "Miracle" status, the Braves were strongly favored to get hammered by Connie Mack's American League champs, the Philadelphia Athletics, in the World Series. After all, the Athletics had their fabled "$100,000 infield" (anchored by Stuffy McInnis – see pages 14-27 – on first), supreme pitching (three of their moundsmen, Eddie Plank, Chief Bender, and Herb Pennock, would go on to Hall of Fame immortality), and the inspired guidance of their manager, Connie Mack. Plus they'd handily defeated the New York Giants four games to one in the Series of 1913. There were, in fact, many baseball folk who predicted the Mackmen would sweep the Braves in four straight. The Braves,

however, had faith in themselves and their manager. Johnny Evers, the team's spirited secondsacker, perhaps said it best. "We'll be out there fighting all the while," he affirmed, going on to add that he was looking forward to the Series: "I think we will show up the Athletics, and it is just what I want to do. They need it."

Johnny was right on the mark. The Braves took the first game, 7-1, as Hank Gowdy hit a single, double, and triple. The Braves took the second game, 1-0, as Bill James went all the way to beat Eddie Plank. The Braves took the third game, 5-4, in what was described as a "nerve-racking struggle" in which Lefty held the Mackmen to but two earned runs and the Bostons triumphed, 5-4, in the twelfth inning. The Braves took the fourth game, 3-1, as Dick Rudolph stilled the Athletics' bats once more. There was no fifth game. The Braves had taken it all...the first time in World Series' history that a team triumphed in four straight. "The best team won," admitted Connie Mack, ever the gentleman (ever the *gentleman New Englander*, it should be noted: Connie was born Cornelius McGillicuddy in East Brookfield, Massachusetts on December 22, 1862).

After 1914, 1915 was almost certain to be a downer. It was. The Braves dropped to second behind the Phillies, and Lefty fell to 10-9. Life on the mound brightened for the southpaw the next season, 1916, however. He finished at 17-10 with a sterling 2.02 ERA. The Braves, though, dropped down another slot, finishing third. A game both the team and Lefty would've preferred to have had rained out was a game against the Giants on May 26. The New Yorkers clobbered the Bostonians, 12-1. Lefty was, in the poetic words of *The New York Times*, "batted all over the lot. As a result," continued *The Times*, "the Braves' fielders got plenty of exercise pursuing the ball here, there, and everywhere." As the season progressed, Lefty, his ineffectual game against the Giants forgotten, settled into a steady groove, notching his most successful season to date. Impressive games abounded. On August 5, our man from Derry shut out the Reds, 1-0, on a five-hitter. On August 11, the portsider pitched in both games of a doubleheader against Pittsburgh, going two innings in a 2-1 loss, and then the full nine in a 4-1 victory. On August 22, he hurled a rain-shortened five-inning win, allowing but one hit, over Cincinnati. On August 29, he held the Pirates to eight scattered hits in a 6-1 win as the Braves battled it out with Brooklyn (the eventual winner) and Philadelphia for the NL crown.

Then there was the game of September 18 in which Lefty, often used as a pinchhitter, drove in both runs as he held St. Louis to three hits in a 2-0 win. And on September 27, he took the Bucs again, in a four-hit, 1-0 masterpiece. Lefty Tyler's game of games for 1916, however, came on September 30. The Braves met the Giants in a doubleheader in front of 38,000 screaming Polo Grounds' fans. The Giants took game number one for their twenty-sixth straight victory! The fans – and the Giants – wanted number twenty-seven in the

nightcap. They didn't get it. In what was melodramatically described as "a shock great as the fall of Troy," the Braves won. And you can probably guess who was on the hill for Boston that day. Wrote *The Times*: "It took the efforts of George Tyler, one of the most formidable left handers in the National League to subdue the bold warriors who make Coogan's Bluff their stomping grounds." When the screaming stopped, the Braves, with a five-run outburst in the seventh, had eight while the Giants had three. (Ed. note: that run of twenty-six straight set by John McGraw and company in 1916 is still, all these decades later, the all-time major league record). There was no doubt about it: 1916 was a fine year for Lefty. He won 17, lost 10, tossed six shutouts (second best in the league), and had that sterling 2.02 ERA.

Lefty's last season in a Boston uniform was 1917. It was not an especially satisfying season for either the southpaw or the team. The lefty finished with a mark of 14-12. The Braves finished sixth. Worth mentioning is that the New Hampshirite, always pretty good with the bat, played eleven games at first base while hitting a credible .231 in 134 at bats.

On January 4, 1918, Lefty was traded to the Cubs as part of a complicated three-club trade. The press called our southpaw "one of the most effective left-handed pitchers in the National League," noting that Charles Weeghman, president of the Cubs (and the man who had built Weeghman Park – now Wrigley Field – as the home of the Chicago Whales of the shortlived Federal League), was

PITCHER

determined to field a "strengthened" team. Mr. Weeghman was certainly doing just that: less than a month earlier he'd acquired almost-perennial 30-game winner Grover Cleveland Alexander (as well as his batterymate, Bill Killefer) from the Phillies.

That the Cubbies took the NL flag in 1918 is impressive. That they took it without Grover Cleveland Alexander is doubly so. Alex went from winning 30 games in 1917 (and 33 in 1916 and 31 in 1915) to winning two games in 1918. The reason: there was a war going on and the legendary pitcher's draft board back home in Nebraska drafted Alexander into the U.S. Army in late April. Grover said he'd prefer the Navy, but the draft board said, "Nope, you're in the Army now." (Ed. note: Grover Cleveland Alexander was shipped out to France on May 31. He returned with the rank of sergeant, a hearing loss, and epileptic seizures. Although he pitched in the bigs until 1930 he was never the same, either as a person or a pitcher, as before the war).

With "Alexander the Great" the Cubs would have been unstoppable. Without him, they were merely good. But good enough to grab first place on June 6 and hold on to it through what was a war-shortened season. As with the Braves in 1914, Lefty Tyler found himself part of a Big Three. Steady 20-game winner James "Hippo" Vaughn went 22-10, Claude Hendrix, who'd won 29 games for the Federal League Whales in 1914, was 19-7. Lefty won 19 and lost 9, while sporting a superfine ERA of 2.00 (second best in the league), striking out 102 (fourth best in the league), tossing eight shutouts (tied for best in the league), and throwing 22 complete games (tied for fourth in the league). With that kind of pitching you don't need a lot of offense. The Cubs' leading hitter was rookie shortstop Charlie Hollocher at .316, followed by Fred Merkle (a solid first-baseman who is best, sadly, recalled for a "bonehead" baserunning mistake he made in 1908) at .297. Chicago's manager was Cambridge, Massachusetts' native Fred Mitchell (real name: Frederick Francis Yapp), in his second season at the helm of the Cubs. Fred later (see page 134) went on to manage the Red Sox.

In 1918's shortened season the Cubs came away with 84 games in the win column. Undoubtedly the hardest earned of those wins was a game against the Phils on July 17. It took 21 innings for the Cubs to take the honors, 2-1. What seems amazing now is that both starting pitchers went the route. All 21 innings. John "Mule" Watson went the 21 for the Phils. George "Lefty" Tyler – as if you didn't know – went the 21 for the Cubs.

The season of 1918 was memorable in a pair of ways. First, there was serious concern that the season would not happen, or that it would be so compromised that it really wouldn't much matter. The war took precedence. Over everything. On the Red Sox, however, there was a gangly 23-year old who was causing people to forget, or at least to minimize, the battles raging "over there." That player's name was, of course, Babe Ruth. And 1918 was the

FRED TYLER

Lefty Tyler had a younger brother who also played – albeit briefly – in the majors. His name was Fred Tyler and he was a catcher. Born in Derry on December 16, 1891, Fred had a trial with Lynn in the New England League in 1911; then played semi-pro; was signed by the Braves in 1914. For the Braves he appeared in 18 games in 1914, batting .333 (eight for 24). He later played for Jersey City, Rochester, Newark, Syracuse, Worcester, Waterbury, and Lawrence before retiring in 1926.

Fred Tyler died in Derry on October 14, 1945.

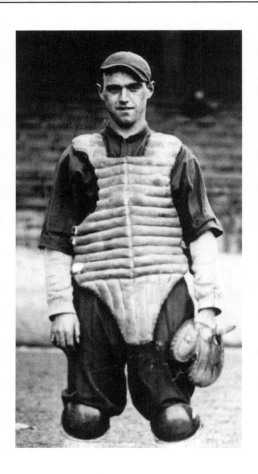

season he began to play the outfield (and some first base, too) as well as pitch. The results were tumultuous. Even though the Babe played for a Boston team, *The New York Times* knew a good thing when they saw one. "Boston Babe Bumps Big Batting Mark" headlined a lengthy article – complete with photos – in the paper's edition of July 21. Continued the article: "He scoffs when he hits a single, merely lifts his eyebrows at a double, begins to take a little interest in life when he hits a triple, and only begins to have a good time when he slams out a home run. That's George Babe Ruth, the caveman of baseball, who is whaling his way to fame this season with the Boston Red Sox."

It was almost inevitable: that the mighty Babe and the Cubs' wondrous pitching should square off at season's end. For king of the World Series hill. The first contest, held in Chicago on September 5, saw Ruth, still taking his turn on the mound, facing Hippo Vaughn. With Ruth in the game, the Sox had their only .300 hitter – at an even .300 – in the line-up. The Cubs had theirs, too, in the person of the aforementioned Charlie Hollocher, at .316. One of the two would go to on to become a legend. The other would go on to become all but completely forgotten.

The Sox took the first tussle. The Babe did the trick. But not with his hitting. No, the

HOME, SWEET "HOME"

The shifting of home parks was fairly common in baseball's earlier years. In 1914 the Braves used Fenway Park as their World Series' home. And in both 1915 and 1916, the Red Sox turned around and made Braves Field their Series' stomping grounds. Carrying on the tradition, the Cubs played their 1918 Series' home contests in Comiskey Park. The reason in each case was, of course, seating capacity. Fenway was bigger than the South End Grounds, the normal abode of the Braves in 1914. When Braves Field came along in 1915 it, likewise, seated more than Fenway. And Comiskey, the White Sox park, was considerably larger seating-wise than Cubs Park (now Wrigley Field).

Lefty chalked up his finest season in 1918, winning 19 games for the Cubs during the regular season and notching another victory as he topped the Red Sox, 3-1 (while driving in two of the Cubs' runs himself), in game two of the World Series.

Circa 1918 photo

PITCHER

Sultan won it his old-fashioned way, taking the mound and stifling his opponents' bats. The Cubs got six scattered singles and no runs. The Red Sox garnered less hits, five, but more runs. Actually, more run. The final score was 1-0, Sox.

Game number two was another low-scoring pitchers' duel. With a different outcome, though. The man from Derry checked the Bosox with six hits. He was also the batting star, singling in two Cub runners in a 3-1 contest. Admired *The Times*: "He (Lefty) soaked (yes, "soaked," not socked) as pretty a single as you ever looked at." There was action off the field, as well. "Coachers" (better known as "coaches" today) Charley Wagner of the Sox and Otto Knabe of the Cubs went at it in the Cubs' dugout after the second inning. The Cubs won that one, too.

Lefty's gem in the second tilt was to be the highlight for the Cubs and their loyal fans. Boston won three of the ensuing four encounters to take the Series, 4-2. Lefty started and went seven innings in both games four and six. In number four, he gave up just three hits but one was a booming triple off the black bat of Babe Ruth (labeled the "Tarzan of Boston" by one sports scribe) that drove in two runs. Final score: Boston, 3 – Chicago, 2. Game number six saw Lefty again on the case, but losing after his rightfielder, Max Flack, committed what was termed "a ludicrous muff" by the press. Max dropped a line drive to allow two Red Sox to cross the plate. Final score: Boston, 2 – Chicago, 1. The Red Sox were once again World Champs. It hasn't happened since.

After his wonderful 1918, big things were expected from Lefty in 1919. Instead he ended up posting a dismal 2-2 record. The cause: bad health. At first it appeared the southpaw was suffering from neuritis in his left shoulder. But extensive tests at the storied Mayo Clinic proved otherwise. George had bad teeth. So bad that all but three of them had to be yanked. Ouch!

Back on the mound in 1920 – with his dentures flying high – Lefty enjoyed his last notable season, hurling 193 innings and posting an 11-12 record.

After a 3-2 mark through mid-season of 1921, Lefty was sent down to Rochester. He pitched intermittently for the Red Wings for the remainder of 1921 and through 1922 before retiring as an active player at the conclusion of the '22 season.

His playing days behind him, George "Lefty" Tyler turned to umpiring: first in the New England League; then in the Eastern League. He later worked for the New England Power Company and, later yet, was a shoe cutter. He died at his home in Lowell, Massachusetts on September 29, 1953.

RAYMOND WILLISTON "RAY" COLLINS,

shown here warming up at Fenway Park circa 1914, was born in Colchester, Vermont on February 11, 1887 and died in Burlington, Vermont on January 9, 1970. Was a ninth-generation descendant of William Bradford of Plymouth Colony fame. Captain of baseball, basketball, and tennis teams at Burlington (Vermont) High School. Then starred on the diamond for the University of Vermont. Pitched Bangor of the Maine State League to pennants, 1907-1908.

Signed by Red Sox in 1909. Hurled for Sox for seven seasons, 1909-1915. Was a southpaw sidearm control pitcher who was 13-11 in 1910, 11-12 in 1911, 13-8 in 1912, 19-8 in 1913, and 20-13 in 1914. Was especially tough on Ty Cobb; once even walking a batter intentionally to get to the Georgia Peach. Tossed six shutouts in 1914, fourth best in league. Demoted to bullpen by pitching-rich Sox, 1915; then offered a contract with substantial pay cut. Retired from pro ball, 1916, to return to Vermont and run family farm. Was head baseball coach at UVM, 1925-1926. Lifetime record is 84-62 with a sparkling 2.51 ERA.

ROBERT MURRAY "BOB" BROWN,
pictured here in his glory year, 1932, was
born in Dorchester, Massachusetts on
April 1, 1911 and died in Pembroke,
Massachusetts on August 3, 1990.
Pitched sparingly for Braves, 1930-1931;
hit peak in 1932 when was 14-7 with tidy
3.30 ERA. Injured pitching arm, 1933,
playing badminton ("a vicious pastime,"
sarcastically penned Harold Kaese in
his 1948 book, THE BOSTON
BRAVES), and was never the same
again. Was 2-13 the remainder of
major league career, 1933-1936.
Lifetime was 16-21 with 4.48 ERA.

**ALVA WILLIAM "AL"/"BEAR
TRACKS" JAVERY,**
pictured here in a 1944 photo,
was born in Worcester, Massachusetts
on June 5, 1918 and
died in Woodstock,
Connecticut on
September 13, 1977.
Spent entire seven-year
big league career, 1940-
1946, with Braves. A
solid 6'3", he saw a
tremendous amount of
work, 1941-1944, when a
medical deferment kept
him out of the service.
Best season was 1943
when won 17 games,
fifth best in league, and
logged 303 innings

pitched, tops in either
league. Won in double
figures all four sea-
sons, 1941-1944 (and,
with a weak team
behind him, lost in
double figures as
well). Nickname "Bear
Tracks" came from his
large feet displacing
chunks of terrain
when he was on the
mound. Lifetime is 53-
74 with a 3.80 ERA.

THOMAS JOSEPH "BUCK" O'BRIEN, shown here in a circa 1912 view, was born in Brockton, Massachusetts on May 9, 1882 and died in Dorchester, Massachusetts on July 25, 1959. A hard-throwing spitballer, he joined the Red Sox in 1911 and peaked, with a record of 20-13 and an ERA of 2.58, in 1912. Was starting Sox pitcher in first major league game ever played at Fenway Park, April 20, 1912. Lost two games in 1912 World Series. Not noted for keeping in shape, O'Brien got off to a 4-9 start in 1913 and was sold to White Sox in July. Was winless for Pale Hose and out of the majors by 1914. Lifetime is 29-25 with a 2.63 ERA.

IRVING MELROSE "IRV"/ "CY THE SECOND" YOUNG, pictured here in a circa 1905 photo, was born in Columbia Falls, Maine on July 21, 1877 and died in Brewer, Maine on January 14, 1935. Pitched in many amateur leagues but didn't turn pro until, in 1904 at age 27, joined Concord (New Hampshire) in the New England League, where was discovered and signed by the Beaneaters (Braves). Led National League in three categories in rookie year, 1905: most innings pitched (378), most games started (42), most complete games (41). Both the innings-pitched and compete game marks are still 20th/21st century major league rookie records. Same year, 1905, won 20 games, with seven shutouts. Only Christy Mathewson had more shutouts that year. He had eight. Alas, however, Irv lost 21 games as Beaneaters posted woeful 51-103 record. Won 16 games, 1906, and ten, 1907, but

received little offensive support and lost 25 and 23, respectively. Traded to Pirates, June, 1908; was 4-3 for Bucs that season. Pitched for Minneapolis in the American Association in 1909, where earned one more shot in majors with the White Sox. With Sox, 1910-1911, was total of 9-14. Continued to toil in minors through 1916. Lifetime in majors is 63-94 with impressive 3.11 ERA.

CHESTER RAYMOND "CHET" NICHOLS, JR.,

pictured here in a 1951 photo, was born in Providence, Rhode Island on February 22, 1931 and died in Lincoln, Rhode Island on March 27, 1995. Was the son of Chet Nichols, Sr. who pitched for Pirates, Giants and Phillies, 1926-1932. Chet, Jr. was 11-8 with league-leading 2.88 ERA for Braves in rookie year, 1951. Then spent two years in service; was never as sharp again. With Milwaukee Braves won 18 but lost 20, 1954-1956. Sent down to minors with arm trouble, 1956. Later, 1960-1963, was with Red Sox as reliever and spot starter. Closed out major league career with three games for Reds, 1964. Lifetime is 34-36 with a 3.64 ERA.

MATTHEW CONSTANTINE "MAX" SURKONT,

shown here in a circa 1950 photo, was born in Central Falls, Rhode Island on June 16, 1922 and died in Largo, Florida on October 8, 1986. Max threw a lot of pitches for a lot of teams. Signed by the Cardinals, he started his pro career with Cambridge (Maryland) in the Eastern Shore League at age 16 in 1938. Went from there to Portsmouth (Ohio), Decatur, and Rochester. After three years in service, 1943-1945, returned to Rochester where remained until drafted by White Sox in December, 1948. Was 3-5 with Chicago, 1949; then traded to Braves for whom enjoyed his best seasons, 1950-1953. Won in double figures, 1951-1953. Peak year was 1953 when went 11-5 with (Milwaukee) Braves. Set a then-record by striking out eight batters in a row against the Reds, May 25, 1953. Was with Pirates 1954-1956. Went on to also pitch for Cardinals, 1956, and Giants, 1957. Lifetime, pitching for primarily weak clubs, is 61-76 with ERA of 4.38.

THEY HAD HEART

The pair of pitchers featured here are included in THE LOST NEW ENGLAND NINE because they were troupers of the first order. Both hurled for the Red Sox when the Sox were horrendous. In 1906, the year

Joe Harris went an unbelievable 2-21, the Sox (actually then called the Pilgrims) were dead last in the American League with a 49-105 record. Joe, in fact, was in select company: teammate Cy Young – *the* Cy Young – also lost 21 games that fruitless year. Curt Fullerton, too, pitched when the Hub Hose were abysmal. When he went 2-15 in his worst season, 1923, the Sox were again dead last, with a mark of 61-91. To pitch for the Red Sox in those days you had to have heart…because you sure weren't going to have runs.

JOSEPH WHITE "JOE" HARRIS, pictured here in a circa 1906 photo, was born in Melrose, Massachusetts on February 1, 1882 and died in Melrose, Massachusetts on April 12, 1966. Pitched three seasons for the Pilgrims/Red Sox, 1905-1907, running up a super-awful 2-21 record, 1906, for a team that was dreadful both offensively and defensively. Highlight was probably a 24-inning duel with Colby Jack Coombs and the Athletics on September 1, 1906. Both moundsmen went the distance before the A's took the contest, not surprisingly, by pushing across three runs in the 24th. Lifetime is 3-30 in spite of a respectable 3.35 ERA.

CURTIS HOOPER "CURT" FULLERTON, looking a little shellshocked in this circa 1923 photo, was born in Ellsworth, Maine on September 13, 1898 and died in Winthrop, Massachusetts on January 2, 1975. He was a stellar moundsman for Mechanic Arts High School, Boston. Signed by the Red Sox in 1921, was sent to Toronto, then in the International League. Was 14-10 with Maple Leafs and brought up to Red Sox late in 1921. Pitched six seasons in the majors, 1921-1925 and 1933, all for Bosox. "Best" season was 1924 when was 7-12. Highlight was being one of but 20 players to appear in Grand Opening Day of Yankee Stadium, April 18, 1923. Lifetime is 10-37 with an ERA of 5.11.

Joe Harris and Curt Fullerton were not alone. Both the Red Sox and the Braves had their share of other hard luck pitchers, too. There was, however, one Boston moundsman who most definitely went from hard luck to good luck. His name was CHARLES "RED" RUFFING. Ruffing, shown here in a 1929 spring training shot, was the Red Sox "stopper" from 1925 until May of 1930, during some of the team's very worst seasons. With Boston, Red "stopped" for 39 victories vs. 96 losses, including 25 losses in 1928 and 22 in 1929. He never had a winning season with the Sox. Then came a trade to the Yankees on May 6, 1930. Things reversed. Red suddenly became a winner. From 1930 through 1946 he won 234 games; lost 129. He also won seven World Series games. Had Red discovered a miraculous new pitch? No, he had discovered a team that scored runs by the drove. Red Ruffing was inducted into the Hall of Fame in 1967. Might Joe and/or Curt have been Cooperstown candidates if they, too, had been traded to a powerhouse club? Yep.

James Francis "Shanty" Hogan

Through the years when it has come to catchers, baseball has come to New England. Fisk, Cochrane, Hartnett, Hegan, Tebbetts, Sukeforth, Carrigan, Perkins, Moran, Mack, Kittredge, Bemis, McLean, Robinson. The list is long and talented. High on that list is Shanty Hogan. High in terms of hitting and backstopping. And high in terms of colorfulness. Noted for his melodic – and powerful – Irish baritone, Shanty would often serenade batters with a chorus of this or that. Traded with another player from the Braves to the Giants for the great Rogers Hornsby in 1928, Shanty was asked by one facetious reporter if he could play second base. "No," replied Shanty, "but I can sing it." And he probably could: Shanty teamed with Giant infielder Andy Cohen as a vaudeville act called *Cohen & Hogan* during the off-season. It was Shanty's weight, though, that ranked especially high. The big guy was generally in the 240-260 range, with a report now and again that he'd topped 300. For many years Shanty would bring his mother, Delia, to spring training to cook for him. "My boy Francis," she would say, "hasn't he a grand appetite?" He certainly had. In his book, THE GIANTS OF THE POLO GROUNDS, author Noel Hynd tells of the restaurant in New York that included four sizes of steak on its menu. Small weighed one pound; medium was two pounds; large was three; last came the king of them all, weighing in at a hefty five pounds. It was called "The Shanty Hogan."

"Shanty" was born James Francis Hogan in Somerville, Massachusetts on March 21, 1906, the son of Irish immigrants Delia and James Hogan. Signed by the Braves as an outfielder right out of Somerville High (also the alma mater of Hod Ford and Deacon Danny MacFayden: see pages 98-99) in 1925, Shanty saw limited service with the Braves that very year. He then saw action with Albany and Worcester, both in the Eastern League, with the parent club again, with Providence, and, finally, with Lynn, in the New England League. It was with Lynn, in 1926, that Shanty exchanged his outfielder's glove for a catcher's glove. He would remain a catcher the rest of his ballplaying years.

In 1927, Shanty alternated with Frank Gibson behind the plate for the Braves, appearing in 71 games and hitting a promising .288. Then came 1928, a year that began with a momentous event in the life of James Francis: he was sent to the New York Giants on January 10 in a trade still considered one of baseball's

CATCHER

Photo, Hot Springs Arkansas, February 1928

It's difficult to tell if John McGraw and his new catcher are shaking hands or squaring off in this February, 1928 spring training photo. During the five years that J. Francis was one of the McGrawmen, the two were almost constantly squabbling. Mostly about Shanty's weight. The press sometimes called Shanty "husky." McGraw – no welterweight himself – called him fat.

most noteworthy swaps. At the time the press labeled Shanty "obscure." Maybe so. But not for long. He and another player, outfielder Jimmy Welsh, had been dealt to the McGrawmen in exchange for Rogers Hornsby: the very same Rogers Hornsby generally considered to be the greatest right-handed hitter of all time.

It was difficult to remain "an unknown," as one newspaper termed Shanty, under the media's spotlight. Plus there was Shanty's bigness. He was generally listed as 6'1" and 240, but there were those who said the 240 was on a diet day. On at least one occasion the Polo Grounds' announcer didn't bother to even use his megaphone to announce Shanty as a pinch hitter. He just walked around the field and drew the fans' attention by pointing. "They all knew it was either Shanty or an elephant," quipped *The New York Times*.

It took some time for Shanty to get rolling that inaugural Giant season. As John Kieran wrote in his *Sports of the Times* column: "He's a big fellow and needs time to work into shape." In the early going Shanty and veteran Bob O'Farrell shared the backstop duties. But from June on it was J. Francis and his powerful bat most every game. Almost as much fun as all his base hits, for Shanty, was that he was on a team that was in a pennant race – and a three-way race at that. Fighting it out for first-place honors were the Cardinals (with Big Jim Bottomley on first, Frankie Frisch at second, Rabbit Maranville at short, Chick Hafey in left, and Jesse Haines, Wee Willie Sherdel and the age-less Grover Cleveland Alexander doing the hurling); the Cubs (with Hack Wilson, Kiki Cuyler, Riggs Stephenson, and New Englander Charles "Gabby" Hartnett providing the firepower, and Pat Malone, John "Sheriff" Blake, Charlie Root, and Guy Bush on the mound); and the Giants (with "Memphis Bill" Terry holding down first, Travis Jackson at short, Freddie Lindstrom at third, Lefty O'Doul in left, slugger Mel Ott in right, our man Shanty behind the plate, and Freddie Fitzsimmons, Larry Benton, and a 24-year old rookie named Carl Hubbell the mainstays on the hill).

The race went well for the McGrawmen through most of the season. Some losses. More wins. As August wound down the Giants were in first place, although by the slenderest of margins. In his *Sports of the Times* column of August 21, John Kieran wrote that the Giants were "riding high." He liked the fact that so many of the Giants' remaining games were to be played at home, in the Polo Grounds. He congratulated McGraw, too, on "picking up Karl (sic) Hubbell, which is something like picking up a wire-wheeled limousine after your kiddie car has skidded off the road." Lastly, he discussed the National League's top catchers, writing "Frank Hogan might be mentioned for his persistent pounding of enemy pitchers and his careful guarding of the home plate against runners coming in from third. Hogan," continued Mr. Kieran, "has a powerful whip, too. But when the subject of base running is brought up," punned the colorful columnist, "Hogan supporters have to start for the exits

CATCHER

WHY "SHANTY" WAS CALLED "SHANTY"

In his *Sports of the Times* column of April 14, 1928, noted *New York Times'* sportswriter John Kieran addressed the question as to why Shanty was called "Shanty." How did James Francis Hogan become Shanty Hogan, a seemingly insulting tag? To be called "Shanty Irish," after all, is hardly a compliment. And "Hogan" is certainly an Irish surname.

When Kieran asked J. Francis the nickname's origin, the new Giant replied, "Aw, I called one of the other birds (players) a 'Dutchman' and he came back at me – with 'Shanty." Did the nickname bother Shanty?, Kieran pressed on. "If I can get base hits I wouldn't care if they called me 'Oswald," responded the weighty receiver.

"IF FRANK HOGAN GROWS
ANY BIGGER"

"Speaking of weight, if Frank Hogan grows
any bigger the umpires behind the plate will
have to sit in the grand stand. Hogan is
already crowding them back to the screen."

The New York Times
September 2, 1928

on their hands and knees."

The Giants would ride high no longer. On August 20, they beat the Reds, 5-3. They then proceeded to lose ten of their next eleven games. It took Shanty's rotund batterymate, "Fat Freddie" Fitzsimmons, to finally halt the slide. Freddie beat the Dodgers, 2-1, on September 1. McGraw's charges then took three more in a row. But it was too late. The Giants' fate was sealed. And that fate was second place. As for J. Frank: the man from Somerville hit a resounding .333 to finish first among all NL catchers and tenth among all NL batsmen. With Jimmy Welsh ending up at .307, the "Hornsby trade" didn't look so bad for the Polo Grounders after all.

Shanty Hogan played four more seasons for the Giants. Of the four, 1930 was the standout. You had to love 1930. Especially if you were a hitter. Even more so if you were a National League hitter. There are those who contend the powers behind baseball had the ball "juiced up" in order to produce more hits, more runs, and, it was hoped, greater attendance. True or not, 1930 was definitely the *Year of the Hitter*. Scores that sounded more like football than baseball abounded. The last National Leaguer to bat .400? Bill Terry, with .401. The all-time record for RBIs in a major league season? The Cubs' Hack Wilson, with a resounding 190. Both happened in 1930. Shanty, Woonsocket-born Gabby Hartnett, New Hampshirite Barney Friberg of the Phils, and Winthrop, Maine's Del Bissonette of the Robins (Dodgers) all hit over .335. None were even in

the Senior Circuit's list of top 15 batters.

In the pennant race, the Robins, Cubs, Giants, and Cards – in that order – were all in the thick of things. It stayed that way, too. In early August, it was still the Robins, Cubs, Giants, and St. Louis. In the race for batting honors it was Bill Terry (.406), Babe Herman (.400), Chuck Klein (.394), Lefty O'Doul (.391), and Riggs Stephenson (.381) heading the pack. Shanty was not too far off the mark, at .352.

By mid-September it was the Cards who had leapfrogged over their opponents to hold down the "sun berth," a name then used for the team on top, with the Robins and Cubs in hot pursuit. *The Times*: "Probably the Giants are out of the pennant race now. But the Robins were out two weeks ago and they climbed right back in again. If it goes on much longer, the Phillies (at the time dead last in the National League with a woeful 48-93 record) may rise up and take a hand in it."

Topsy-turvy season that it was, the Giants did not come back to take the flag. (Neither did the Phils!). No, the Cardinals held on. Never mind that the Cubs' Hack Wilson went wild with 56 home runs and those unbelievable 190 RBIs. Never mind that Brooklyn had its best season since 1920. The Redbirds had their own heroes. Players with names like Frisch (.346), Hafey (.336), and Bottomley (.304). A rookie outfielder named George Watkins hit at a .373 clip. And a pitcher known as Jerome "Dizzy" Dean, just up from Houston in the Texas League, stopped the Pirates cold with a three-hitter in the last game of the regular season.

The Giants, meanwhile, had to be content to share in the glory of their teammate, Bill Terry. All the firstsacker did was tie the (still) all-time National League record for hits in a season with a hefty 254. And bat .401, the last player to bat .400 or more in the Senior Circuit. All the media attention there was – and there wasn't much – focused on Terry's base-hit output. It was mentioned now and again that, by batting over .400, Memphis Bill would pretty much assure himself of the batting crown, but that was about it. (Ed. note: It *had* only been five years, though, since the Rajah, Rogers Hornsby, had recorded a .403 mark). Strangely enough, the Giants had several open dates at the very end of their season. Today that sort of break in the action would assure that much more drama, that much more media coverage. But not then. On one of the off-days the McGrawmen traveled up the Hudson to play an exhibition game against the Sing Sing nine. The tilt was an annual affair, but there was no home and away. The contest was always, not surprisingly, played on the inmates' diamond. (The inmates, incidentally, pushed across six runs in the bottom of the ninth to take the game, 6-5).

Back in New York City, Terry went one for four against the Phils on September 27 to tie Lefty O'Doul's National League high of 254. The next day, in the Giants' final game of the season, he went 0 for 5. The result: O'Doul kept his name in the record book and Terry's average dropped to .401. (Ed. note: every major leaguer who's stepped up to the plate since – save for the Splendid Splinter, Ted Williams, in 1941 – should have to worry about ending the season by *dropping* to .401!).

Shanty Hogan had enjoyed five very satisfying seasons as a Giant. He racked up batting averages of .339 (1930); .333 (1928); .301 (1931); .300 (1929); and .287 (1932). For four of those five seasons – the first four – the New Yorkers were pennant contenders. In 1932, however, the team fell to sixth: definitely not pennant-contention material. The result was a managerial change. The ailing John McGraw, in his thirty-third year as a big league manager, was replaced by Bill Terry, he of .401 fame, on June 3. There was also a host of changes made at season's end. Shanty was one of those changes. On December 29, the veteran catcher was dealt back to his former team, the Braves, for a reported $25,000.00. As could have been predicted, the media had a field day. Reported *The Times*: "With one flourish of a pen they (the Giants) unloaded Frank Hogan, mastodonic catcher, onto the Boston Braves, and if nothing else was accomplished it at least assured the Giants of considerably lighter traveling next season." The article went on to highlight the run-ins J. Frank had had with his manager. Season after season McGraw had kept after J. Frank to slim down. "On one occasion," continued *The Times* reporter, "McGraw was quite pleased, upon noticing Hogan's meal checks, that Frank was ordering only dainty vegetable dishes." McGraw's pleasure diminished considerably, however, when

CATCHER

This is number 30 in a set of 240 cards issued by the Goudey Gum Company, makers of Big League Chewing Gum, in 1933. On the back of the card it is noted "Here's big Frank Hogan, catcher of the Braves. He's a hard hitter, when he lands on the ball." Although oddly phrased, the words made their point: the beefy backstopper could hit.

Greatly enlarged (actual size is 2³/₈" x 2⁷/₈") Big League card, 1933

he later learned that, by special arrangement with the kitchen, each of Shanty's "dainty" dishes was code for a decidedly non-dainty item. "Spinach" was code for porterhouse steak. "Broccoli" meant boiled potatoes. "Lettuce" translated to apple pie à la mode. The big guy was determined to remain big.

In announcing Shanty's move back to Boston, the Associated Press was a little kinder. It merely stated that "The Boston Braves will have to provide food for Frank Hogan's gar-gantuan appetite during the 1933 National League season." As for Shanty himself, the 1933 edition of WHO'S WHO IN MAJOR LEAGUE BASEBALL probably had it right when it wrote: "He (Shanty) hated to say farewell to Manhattan but rather welcomed the assignment to play in Boston, which is just around the corner from his beloved Somerville."

The rotund receiver played three years for the Braves his second time around. While his

Circa 1934
photo

CATCHER

When Shanty was sold back to the Braves by the Giants in December 1932 the Associated Press commented that now it would be up to the Braves "to provide food for Hogan's gargantuan appetite." It was true. But Shanty repaid the club and then some by catching 121 straight errorless games from May 17, 1933 through August 4, 1934. It was a record and one that, as pointed out by Harold Kaese in his classic 1948 book, THE BOSTON BRAVES, "had nothing to do with eating."

storied weight held up, however, his batting average did not. Shanty dropped to .253 in 1933 and .262 in 1934, before rebounding to .301 in 1935. He played less, too: 95 games as a catcher in 1933; 90 in 1934; 56 in 1935.

J. Frank did a lot of moving about the remainder of his pro career. He bounced to Minneapolis (American Association) after being released by Boston in July 1935. Then it was on to Albany (International League); a quick visit back to the bigs with the Washington Senators (for whom he hit .323 in 19 games in 1936); Indianapolis (American Association); Toronto (International); and his last shot with the Senators, at the end of the 1937 season. He played some, too, with San Diego (Pacific Coast) before tossing in the chest protector with Springfield (Eastern League) in 1939.

His baseball days behind him, James Francis Hogan spent most of his time in and around Somerville. During World War II he worked as a rigger in a nearby shipyard. "The swellest thing about working in a shipyard," said Shanty, obviously reflecting back to his many run-ins with John McGraw, "is that you never get fined."

Shanty Hogan died in Faulkner Hospital in Medford, Massachusetts on April 7, 1967. In his obituary it was written "He had a .295 batting average in the big leagues and a 1.000 mark in the Grocery League."

The big guy would have liked that.

PATRICK JOSEPH "PAT" MORAN, shown here in a circa 1906 photo, was born in Fitchburg, Massachusetts on February 7, 1876, and died in Orlando, Florida on March 7, 1924. During his big league career, 1901-1914, was generally a second-string catcher who played some infield, too. Was with the Beaneaters (Braves), 1901-1905; Cubs, 1906-1909; Phillies, 1910-1914. Best season, 1903, when hit .262 and slammed out 7 homers – tied for second-highest in league – in only 389 at-bats. Hit three triples in game against Pirates in August 1905. Later managed Phillies and Reds to pennants. Lifetime as player is .235 in 819 games.

WILLIAM FRANCIS "BILL"/"ROUGH" CARRIGAN, depicted here on a 1912 Hassan Cigarettes' card, was born in Lewiston, Maine on October 22, 1883 and died in Lewiston, Maine July 8, 1969. Star in both football and baseball in high school. Next came stardom, again in both sports, at Holy Cross. Signed by Red Sox, Carrigan became a skilled handler of pitchers. Especially noted for blocking the plate, which earned him his "Rough" nickname. Went on to become a manager of distinction (see pages 128-133). Lifetime, in a playing career that spanned 1906-1916, is .257 in 706 games.

EUGENE ABRAHAM "GENE"/ "RED" DESAUTELS, pictured here in a 1937 photo, was born in Worcester, Massachusetts on June 13, 1907 and died on November 5, 1994 in Flint, Michigan. After college at Holy Cross served four clubs as strong-on-defense/weak-at-bat catcher, starting with Tigers in 1930 and running through the Athletics in 1946. In between came Red Sox, 1937-1940, and Indians, 1941-1943 and 1945. Best season was 1938 when hit solid .291 with 16 doubles in 108 games for Sox. Lifetime is .233 in 712 games.

GEORGE ROBERT "BIRDIE" TEBBETTS,

shown here in a June 1937 photo, was born in Burlington, Vermont on November 10, 1912 and died in Bradenton, Florida on March 24, 1999. His distinctive nickname reportedly came from his youth, when an aunt was said to have remarked, "He chirps like a bird." A skilled and shrewd receiver – "Fine catcher" is how Maine catching legend Clyde Sukeforth summed up Birdie – Tebbetts was a star at Nashua (New Hampshire) High School and Providence College (where he earned a bachelor's degree in philosophy) before turning pro in 1934. Played fourteen years in the majors, 1936-1952, with three years out for military service, 1943-1945. Biggest year was 1940, when batted .296 and helped guide his first team, the Tigers, into the World Series. Next, 1947-1950, came the team he'd wanted from the start, the Red Sox. Last, 1951-1952, came the Indians. Later managed Cincinnati, Milwaukee, and Cleveland. Lifetime as a player is .270 in 1162 games.

Success has its rewards. Here's Birdie, left, and Tigers' secondbaseman – and future Hall-of-Famer – Charlie Gehringer off on a West Indies cruise, October 19, after winning the 1940 pennant.

MANAGER

William Francis "Bill"/"Rough" Carrigan

Who was their manager the last time the Red Sox won two pennants in a row? Who was their manager the last time (and the *only* time) the Red Sox won two World Series in a row? The answer to both questions is, of course, Bill Carrigan. "Rough" – his nickname came from the aggressive manner in which he would block the plate during his backstopping days – graduated from being the Sox catcher to being their manager. He had done a splendid job with the former. He was even more successful with the latter. The man who helped mold a skinny – yes, skinny – kid from the streets of Baltimore into "the Babe" also guided the Hub Hose to American League championships in both 1915 and 1916. And then on to World Championships, too, by defeating the Phillies in 1915 and the Dodgers in 1916.

Catchers make good managers. They're used to handling pitchers. So why not handle the whole team? Just look at the list: Connie Mack, Wilbert "Uncle Robbie" Robinson, Buck Martinez, Paul Richards, Wes Westrum, Gabby Hartnett, Al Lopez, Mickey Cochrane, Jimmie Wilson, Pat Moran (see page 126), Luke Sewell, Steve O'Neill, George "The Miracle Man" Stallings, Pat Corrales, Del Crandall,

Yogi Berra, Birdie Tebbetts (see page 127), Ralph Houk, Buck Rodgers, others. (In fact, as I write this – in the spring of 2003 – an amazing nine of the 30 men now managing in the majors are former catchers. How many can you name?).

William Francis "Bill"/"Rough" Carrigan was a catcher (see page 126), and a good one. Born in Lewiston, Maine on October 22, 1883, Bill was a double-threat athlete, starring at both baseball and football through grade school and at Lewiston High, too. It was then on to Holy Cross, in Worcester, where Bill continued his athletic achievements. In football he was a halfback. In baseball he started as an infielder, but under Holy Cross coach Tommy McCarthy he became a catcher. And it was Bill's skillful work behind the plate that landed him a contract with the Red Sox in 1906.

Bill, in his years of catching for the Red Sox, was a defensive gem. But he was a pesky hitter as well. Although he never led the league in any offensive category, the Mainer was a respected clutch hitter. In his first shot with Boston, in 1906, he batted a dismal .211. But after a year of seasoning with Toronto, then in the International League, the square-jawed Carrigan arrived to stay. His two best years with the stick were 1909 when he hit .296 and 1911 when he had a .289 mark. Lifetime he was .257. We are not, however, here to rhapsodize about Bill Carrigan's proficiency with

MANAGER

RED SOX STARS

WILLIAM CARRIGAN
BOSTON AMERICAN
CATCHER
KNOCKING OUT A TIMELY HIT

SUPPLEMENT
TO
BOSTON SUNDAY POST

The Pride of Lewiston was there, as a player, the day they opened Fenway Park on April 20, 1912. A little more than a year later he would be the club's manager.

Bill Carrigan as depicted in a supplement to the Boston Sunday Post, 1909

Cover, **The National Police Gazette***, October 28, 1916*

Best Pictures of the World's Series

THE NATIONAL POLICE GAZETTE.

THE LEADING ILLUSTRATED SPORTING JOURNAL IN THE WORLD.

COPYRIGHT FOR 1916, BY RICHARD K. FOX PUBLISHING COMPANY, THE FOX BUILDING, FRANKLIN SQUARE, NEW YORK CITY.

RICHARD K. FOX President and Editor

NEW YORK: SATURDAY, OCTOBER 28, 1916.

VOLUME CIX.—No. 2046 Price 10 Cents

(C) by Underwood & Underwood.

WILBERT ROBINSON AND "BILL" CARRIGAN.

BROOKLYN MANAGER CONGRATULATES RIVAL ON HIS VICTORY IN THE WORLD'S CHAMPIONSHIP SERIES.

Bill being congratulated by Brooklyn manager Wilbert Robinson after the Red Sox had taken their second straight World's Championship, in 1916. A New England native – he was born in Bolton, Massachusetts in 1863 – "Uncle Robbie" won two pennants and no World Series in his 18 years at the helm of the Robins/Dodgers.

the bat and glove. We are here to talk about his reign as the man at the helm. The man where the buck stopped. Red Sox management liked, seemingly, to see skippers come and go in those early years of the team's history. From 1906 until Bill took over in 1913, the Bosox played under no less than nine managers. In one season alone, 1907, the club saw four helmsmen come and go (and they still finished seventh) and, even though Jake Stahl led the team, in 1912, to its first flag in eight years (and a stirring four-games-to-three victory over the Giants in the World Series, too), he was axed before the 1913 season was out. On July 15, with the team at 39-41 and in fifth place, Jake was asked to vacate Fenway Park. Selected to take his place was, of course, Lewiston Bill Carrigan. Under Bill, the club won 40, lost 30, and moved up a notch, to fourth.

In 1914, with the ballclub under Bill's leadership the entire season, the Red Sox finished a strong second to Connie Mack's powerhouse Athletics. That was the year a slender lad by the name of George Herman Ruth made his appearance in the major leagues. The Babe had arrived. And he arrived as a member of the Red Sox...as a left-handed pitcher. Much of his later success – which, alas, came with the Yankees – stemmed from the care and tutoring he received from Bill Carrigan. As Bill would later write in a series of articles for the *Boston Daily Record*: "Nobody could have made Ruth the great pitcher and the great hitter he was but himself. He made himself with the aid of his God-given talents. But," continued Bill,

"breaking in, he had to be disciplined to save him from probably being his own worst enemy. And I saw to it that he was disciplined." Bill even went so far as to room with Babe – and the team's other irrepressible young hurler, Dutch Leonard – to ensure that the fun-loving Ruth didn't overdo the fun. In short, Bill became as much a father figure as a manager. It paid off. Ruth developed into one of the game's premier lefties under squire Bill, helping the Sox take pennants – and World Championships – in both 1915 and 1916. Ruth was 18-8 in 1915; an even more dazzling 23-12, with a league-leading ERA of 1.75, in 1916.

Bill had similar success with the rest of the club. As sportswriters of the period were quick to point out, Bill was not a flashy leader or a driver in the strict sense of the word. Rather, he was a hard worker himself, and his players tended to follow by example. He was also a keen student of the game, possessing an uncanny savvy for knowing what to do when. At no time was this more evident than in Bill's back-to-back World Championships. In the Fall Classic of 1915, his charges were matched against a strong Phillies team that had won the National League crown by seven games. Led by the pitching of Grover Cleveland Alexander (31-10, with a miniscule 1.22 ERA), the slugging of former Red Soxer Gavvy Cravath (24 homers and 115 RBIs, both tops in the majors), and the managing of Fitchburg, Massachusetts' native Pat Moran, they appeared to be tough. They weren't. After the Phils took the first game, 3-1, on an eight-hitter by Alexander, the Sox swept to victory by taking the next four in a row.

It could be said, incidentally, that even the president of the United States came out to watch Bill's handiwork. On October 9, president Woodrow Wilson was on hand as the Sox won their first game of the Series, and their first-ever for "Rough," 2-1. It was a first not only for Bill: it was also the first time a president ever witnessed a World Series' contest.

The second of Bill's successive World Championships, in 1916, was more of the same. The Red Sox faced a Brooklyn ballclub featuring the likes of Jake Daubert, Zack Wheat, and an outfielder named Casey Stengel…and proceeded to also polish them off four games to one. In game number four, manager Carrigan even inserted catcher Carrigan – who'd batted but 63 times all season – behind the plate…and with good results: the player/manager went two for three with an RBI as the Sox won, 6-2. (Note: for more on the Series of 1915 and 1916, please see pages 56-57).

At age 32, riding on top of the world, Lewiston's favorite son decided to call it quits after his rather remarkable 1915 and 1916 triumphs. Actually, he had announced his retirement in early September, so that topping the Robins (as the Dodgers were then called) in the Series just served as an exclamation point for Bill's goodbye. He'd decided that he wanted to spend more time at home. So home to Lewiston it was, there to find considerable success in both real estate (Bill was half-owner of a string of movie theatres spread throughout New England) and banking. Bill had also made no bones about being weary of the constant traveling that baseball requires. As he wrote in a series of 1943 articles entitled *My Days With the Red Sox,* "I was in my thirties, was married and had an infant daughter. I wanted to spend more time with my family than baseball would permit."

By the mid-1920s, however, Bill found himself increasingly restless. He'd sold his movie chain shares at a hefty profit, allowing him to be a gentleman of leisure. It was a role he did not relish. The Red Sox, meanwhile, had fallen upon exceedingly hard times: in the five-year period between 1922 and 1926 they finished last four times and next-to-last the other. They were dreadful. Bob Quinn, who'd bought the franchise in the winter of 1923-24, talked Bill out of retirement. Bill shouldn't have listened. Good manager or not, nothing he could do made much of a difference. Never one to pass the buck, Bill would nevertheless later admit that his players just didn't have it. As he penned in an article in the July 1929 issue of *Baseball Magazine,* "Fighting spirit alone won't make a ball club into a pennant winner. You've got to have batting punch and fielding ability and steady pitching."

After three seasons, 1927-1929, of almost total frustration – and last-place finishes – Bill reluctantly tossed in the towel. He retired from the Red Sox for good. Back in Lewiston, he became a highly successful banker, eventually rising to the post of president of Peoples

MANAGER

Savings Bank.

Bill Carrigan passed away in his beloved Lewiston on July 8, 1969. He was 85. Honest, dependable, hard-working: those were the trademarks of "Old Rough." When, in 1946, he was told that he'd been named to baseball's Honor Roll – a supplement to the Hall of Fame established to pay tribute to outstanding managers, sportswriters and club executives – he responded: "Well, well, that's fine, thank you. Now I've got to get back to the bank."

Photo, October 1916

Bill Carrigan was called a "genius (especially at getting the most out of pitchers)" by noted baseball author Frederick G. Lieb, and "The leader of the red-hosed warriors of the Bailiwick of Beans" by his hometown Lewiston Evening Journal. *Bill was both. And his smiling face beaming forth here seems a splendid way to wind down THE LOST NEW ENGLAND NINE. I hope its pages have caused you to smile some, too.*

FREDERICK FRANCIS "FRED" MITCHELL,

shown here in a formal portrait taken while playing for Phillies in 1903, was born in Cambridge, Massachusetts on June 5, 1878 and died in Newton, Massachusetts on October 13, 1970. Was born "Frederick Francis Yapp," but changed last name to "Mitchell," his mother's maiden name, to avoid being made fun of. If experience gained via playing different positions made one a better manager, Fred Mitchell would have been a manager supreme. Played in 202 big league games, spread across six teams, 1901-1905, 1910 and 1913. Appeared in 97 of them as pitcher, 68 as catcher, 16 as firstbaseman, two or more at every other position. Managed Cubs, 1917-1920; led them to pennant in war-shortened season of 1918, then lost to Red Sox in last Sox World Championship victory. With Cubs is said to have invented in 1918 what later, against Ted Williams, became known as the "Boudreau Shift." (Mitchell's shift was against another Williams: Cy Williams.) Moved from Cubs to Braves after 1920 season. Managed Braves to fourth place in 1921; then dropped to eighth, 1922, and seventh, 1923. Left Braves after 1923 season to accept job of baseball coach at Harvard, a post he held until 1939. Lifetime major league managerial record is 494-543.

Wonder" – and lived up to both in a sadly injury-prone and short career. His 25 home runs in 1928 is the all-time *Brooklyn* Dodger rookie record. He drove in over 100 runs in 1928 and 1930, batting .320 that first season and .336 the latter. Retired, 1933, after suffering both a torn Achilles tendon and blood poisoning, with but four and a fraction seasons under his belt, all with Brooklyn. Went on to manage Des Moines, Bradford (Pennsylvania), Hartford and, in the big time, the Braves, in 1945. Del's stay at the helm in Braves Field, though, was to be short. He replaced Bob Coleman on July 30 when the team was 42-49 and mired in seventh, and guided the squad to a 25-36 mark, good enough to propel the team from seventh to sixth. It was not good enough, however, to keep Braves' management from replacing Del with Billy Southworth at season's end. The Winthrop Wonder later also managed the Portland Pilots (in his home state of Maine), the Toronto Maple Leafs, and Trois Rivières (Quebec). In 1954 he was again offered the job as Braves' manager, but declined, saying he'd rather stay home in Maine.

From a Maine point of view no book on New England ballplayers would in any way be complete without the inclusion of **ADELPHIA LOUIS "DEL" BISSONETTE.** Born in Winthrop, Maine on September 6, 1899 and died in Augusta, Maine on June 9, 1972, he is shown here in a 1945 photo. Had two nicknames – "The Babe Ruth of Maine" and "The Winthrop

BIBLIOGRAPHY/SOURCES

Allen, Lee. THE AMERICAN LEAGUE STORY, New York City: Hill & Wang, 1962.

Anderson, Will. WAS BASEBALL REALLY INVENTED IN MAINE?, Portland, Maine: Anderson & Sons' Publishing Co., 1992.

Asinof, Eliot. EIGHT MEN OUT, New York City: Holt, Rinehart and Winston, 1963.

Carter, Craig. TAKE ME OUT TO THE BALL PARK, St. Louis: The Sporting News Publishing Co., 1983

Chadwick, Bruce. THE BOSTON RED SOX, New York City: Abbeville Press, 1992.

Gold, Eddie and Ahrens, Art. THE GOLDEN ERA OF THE CUBS, Chicago: Bonus Books, 1955.

Golenbock, Peter. FENWAY, New York City: G.P. Putnam's Sons, 1992.

Graham, Frank. THE BROOKLYN DODGERS, New York City: G.P. Putnam's Sons, 1945.

Gropman, Donald. SAY IT AIN'T SO, JOE, Boston: Little, Brown and Company, 1979.

Hirshberg, Al. THE BRAVES, THE PICK AND THE SHOVEL, Boston: Waverly House, 1948.

Honig, Donald. BASEBALL WHEN THE GRASS WAS REAL, New York City: Coward, McCann & Geoghegan, 1975.

Hynd, Noel. THE GIANTS OF THE POLO GROUNDS, New York City: Doubleday, 1988.

Kaese, Harold. THE BOSTON BRAVES, New York City: G.P. Putnam's Sons, 1948.

LaBlanc, Michael L. PROFESSIONAL SPORTS TEAM HISTORIES: BASEBALL, Detroit: Gale Research Inc., 1994.

Lieb, Frederick G. CONNIE MACK: GRAND OLD MAN OF BASEBALL, New York City: G.P. Putnam's Sons, 1945.

Lieb, Frederick G. THE BOSTON RED SOX, New York City: G.P. Putnam's Sons, 1947.

Lieb, Frederick G. THE STORY OF THE WORLD SERIES, New York City: G.P. Putnam's Sons, 1949.

Luhrs, Victor. THE GREAT BASEBALL MYSTERY, South Brunswick, New Jersey: A.S. Barnes and Co., Inc., 1966.

Obojski, Robert. BUSH LEAGUE, New York City: Macmillan Publishing Co., 1975.

Simon, Tom. GREEN MOUNTAIN BOYS OF SUMMER, Shelburne, Vermont: New England Press, 2000.

Smith, Robert. BASEBALL IN THE AFTERNOON, New York City: Simon & Schuster, 1993.

Smith, Ron. THE SPORTING NEWS CHRONICLE OF BASEBALL, New York City: BDD Illustrated Books, 1993.

Plus THE BIG THREE

The by-player files at the A. Bartlett Giamatti Research Center, Baseball Hall of Fame Library, Cooperstown, New York.

THE BASEBALL ENCYCLOPEDIA (Reichler, Joseph L. New York City: Macmillan Publishing Co., 1985 edition).

The New York Times, intermittently, 1901-1945. (I would have much preferred *The Boston Globe*. The nearest source for *The Globe* on microfilm, however, was over 130 miles away: not at all feasible. As it was, I made virtually daily trips – close to 100 – to the nearby Hawthorne-Longfellow Library at Bowdoin College to steep myself in the box scores and baseball commentary that embellish the pages of their *Times* on microfilm. Thank you, Bowdoin.).

PHOTOGRAPH/GRAPHIC CREDITS

INDEX